ONE FOOT
in the
RIGHT
DIRECTION

Bipolar a mental health problem

JANET DUNNE

AuthorHouse™ UK
1663 Liberty Drive
Bloomington, IN 47403 USA
www.authorhouse.co.uk
UK TFN: 0800 0148641 (Toll Free inside the UK)
UK Local: 02036 956322 (+44 20 3695 6322 from outside the UK)

This book is printed on acid-free paper.

ISBN: 979-8-8230-9008-7 (sc)
ISBN: 979-8-8230-9009-4 (e)

Library of Congress Control Number: 2024920726

Print information available on the last page.

Published by AuthorHouse 09/24/204

authorHOUSE®

Acknowledgement's

A very big Thank you for this book goes to my mother Frances, and all my family for loving me. Another to all my friends that have been here and shared my journey. Another to the people who I reached out to when I needed help . another to Margaret, a big Thank you for being who you are, you made me laugh when life wasn't funny at all thank you. Finally a very big thank you to my Job that sustained me through my darkest days and never sacking me, thank you. A big Thank you to the people that have helped me produce this. I could do nothing without the help I have received. But the biggest Thanks goes to the reader that I don't know, You. I Pray that this will help someone else, someone like me.

Overview of my life and my thinking

Hello, my name is Janet Dunne, I come from a town in Dublin called Ballymun. I was born on the 2nd of January 1966. My mother and father split up when I was three years old, and we never seen our father again. He became a missing person. He was sadly missed by his family especially my grandmother. She spent years talking about my father and she never understood why he stayed away. She took this to her grave. I missed not having a father, so my childhood was a bittersweet experience. When I was a child, I secretly hoped my father would come home but that never happened.

I was a chatty little child, it was often said to me, "you're always looking for attention ". This was so true I always had to be amused. When I had nobody to play with, I would go to the nearest adult and start a conversation or ask questions so that they would speak with me. My Granny Kelly one day said to me, "Janet, why don't you go out to the garden and see what the little bees were doing" and off I went, I found a little bee at a flower rubbing his back leg as he did his work hovering over the Flower.

At school I struggled with reading and spelling. In fact, my earliest memory of writing numbers is that all of the numbers were backwards except 8 and 1. It took me years to learn to read. I didn't understand the sounds of words. Even to this day reading unfamiliar words can be hard for me. It is a form of dyslexia but back then you were considered stupid and your only aspirations in life were to become a mammy and have children.

My mother worked in a local factory during my childhood, and she worked with heavy machinery. In the evenings after she made dinner and cleaned the kitchen she would lie down on the couch and sleep while Sandra, Thomas and I would run out to play until we would be called in to go to bed. That's a sweet memory.

Things were not perfect in our household, but it wasn't bad. I struggled with school, so I decided not to go. I went on the hop for four weeks. After a while my sister realized what I was doing, and she decided to go on the hop too!

This came to the attention of the school, and they contacted my mother, and she had to take the day off work. When Sandra and I returned home-to our surprise our mother greeted us at the door with a very nasty look on her face. We had our school bags, and we were pretending at 2:30 to be coming in from school. We never expected to see our mother at the door, so we knew something was up. I don't remember my mother saying anything to us. But my mother took another day off work.

The next day we were taken by my mother to the school principal, she had a lot to say to us. She explained that when children are being reared by a mother on her own, they will be sent to a school away from their family if they do not go to school.

The conversation was so serious and what we had done was so bad. I never went on the hop again. I was too afraid too. I did not enjoy primary school but when I got to secondary school my reading had improved. In secondary school every 40 minutes you had a different teacher. You learnt new subjects, that's when I started to enjoy going to school. I lived for my art and music classes.

A few things happened when I was 13. I made my confirmation that year, my Ma got into a serious relationship, after a few months he moved into our flat and in the August my mother's mother died. I changed school and started the Ballymun Comprehensive School. So, life changed for me. This was the first time I experienced death. I was awfully close to my mother's mother. I grieved her death for many years. I really missed my granny. She was the one person in my life that utterly understood me.

I spent a lot of time at her house. A lot of my weekends were spent in Ballyfermot baking, polishing, asking questions and going to mass with my Gran father. My granny had a bad heart, and she couldn't walk very far. My granny showed me how to do things. She let me sew on her pedal sewing machine upstairs. She let me potter around her house looking in all the drawers and presses. I'd ask her questions like: "Granny what was it like in the olden days, what were you like when you were a child?" and she'd tell me little stories.

When I was 15 my brother Phillip was born but at that stage the relationship between my mother and her boyfriend had become abusive. We were never hurt physically but it greatly affected my understanding of life.

To cope with all of the upset I separated myself by being a teenager. My mother did her best, but she stayed in this relationship for many years. In my opinion, I think she didn't want to see another child been reared without a father. Maybe it seems like I am painting a very bad picture, but it wasn't all bad.

I was out with my friends having a good time. I was in a youth club for many years, and we had a great time with all the teenagers. I had a bike, and I would cycle everywhere with my best friend Paula. We would go on adventures up the Wicklow mountains. We would go out to Donabate and cycle around the coast or just to the Phoenix Park and cycle around. When we weren't doing that, we were with our gang of friends hanging around. Saturday nights we went to the Blind Disco in Drumcondra. I also cycled to my cousins to visit for the day, or I would stay over with them. We were having a ball, I had great fun. I babysat for money to buy my things, and I got pocket money every week from my mother. Always fed and not neglected and lots of good memories too.

The problems of Anxiety were there a little in my childhood because I had no Dad, and I couldn't read like all my peers. Children can be very cruel saying things like "Ha ha ha you've no Dad." "Look at her she can't read." Just point blank tell you, you were stupid because you have to go to the special class.

This did affect me but with my friends and cousins that never happened, just in school. My life made compensation's. I was good at art and making things and I was good at cleaning, so I helped my Ma and my Granny because I helped, I always got sweets or money.

I was always great with children. I loved having fun and playing games. If there was a long conversation going on, I would go and play with my younger cousins. When you have Dyslexia, you can hold conversations one to one easier but when it comes to talking in groups my brain does not work that fast to keep up with the changing topics. I often would go and do something, like have a game of football. Now I am talking about 40 years ago. Today I tend to listen and just come in, with a one liner. The problem is I tend to think about what the people are saying, and I lose the flow of the conversation. I understand it today but years ago I did not.

When I stepped out from my teenage years and into my adult life I was in charge. I wasn't going to do this; I wasn't going to do that; I was never going to accept abuse in my life. I thought I knew the right formula to have a nice life, I was truly afraid at the same time.

How can you take the lead of a situation, take control and be afraid of life going wrong at the same time? Well from my history and my experience I made a lot of decisions and from the people in my life I would do and say what they would say in that situation. I always panicked when things would go wrong.

You see, I was good at cleaning, saving to get something and paying my bills but I knew absolutely nothing about life, love, marriage, unconditional love or loving yourself, these were only things we say. What did they mean? It has taken me all my life to figure them out.

The big joke is that I thought I was right then, but I was so wrong. Now I know nothing much and I take one day as it comes along.

Drama? Yes, I wore the big t-shirt. You could suck me into any drama, and I'd start acting. I'm now saying it was acting because I would be in the thick of it. Saying someone else's opinions and using someone else's words to get the point across that I was right. I don't like saying all this about myself but it's true.

Another T- shirt I had put on when it suited me was to be everyone's little helper. Can you just imagine the lengths I went to, to earn the right to wear that T- shirt? I told you that I was good at cleaning. Yes, it was so bad that my sister's children would say, "Here comes the cleaning lady". I was also good at saving. I had to learn that the hard way too. Not trying to insult my family but I was the family Meddler. I poked my nose into every problem and got myself involved. Well, you must put your money where your mouth is, so I'd have to say goodbye to my savings to help. The problem would be solved, and I'd have no money for myself so to speak.

Basically, I take full blame for my actions, my words of wisdom and advice. Back when I lived a life of full drama. In what I know now, what I did not know then, it's all such a joke hindsight and it makes me laugh today when I think about it all.

The biggest joke is that I am putting what I learnt down on paper in the hope that my story might help you. You may find that what I am talking about is not the way that you want to go with your Bipolar, but I will put the things that I learnt down on paper because they truly helped me in the end.

In truth if I had not gotten Bipolar I more than likely would never have changed. I was oblivious to the fact that I needed to change. I enjoyed the way I was. Just the more I helped the less time I had for my life and my own needs. I was a bag of stress running from pillar to post. I thought when there was a problem that other people's problems were bigger than mine and I allowed myself to forget about me, my needs and wants.

It all got very crazy at times, it is hard to write and not say the stories or the circumstances. They involve other people, people that I care about. As I put myself in their problems it was all my own fault anyway.

A lot of people have problematic lives. We all have times when things do not run smoothly but everyone does not end up where I did. Funnily enough I was able to deal with my problems, it was the problems of others that tipped me over.

My marriage ended in divorce. It started good and ended badly, there were two people in the marriage. I was depressed in the marriage; it did not look like depression as I was active and functioning fine. I did seek help twice in the form of Marriage guidance and Acupuncture to get balanced. Both helped but they just prolonged the solution.

If you have been diagnosed with bipolar, you have been affected by bipolar disorder, but bipolar disorder is not you. We probably share similar experiences with highs and lows, elation and depression. These are feelings that we have, we feel elated when we get happy, we feel depressed when we are sad.

The good news is that we can change how we deal with our highs and lows.

I never really liked listening to people that only talked about their problems. In my life you just had to get on with life and enjoy what you do have. That was my attitude from early, you're not good at this, but you are good at that, you don't have this, but you do have that, because that had been my life.

Counseling didn't agree with me, peeling the onion of your life. Going through the years of your life, this just didn't sit with me. I did go but why did I feel so bad after the session? On the third session I was searching my mind, what will I talk about this week.

This just did not sit with me at all. I also went to self-help groups. I am sorry If you get something from them, but I didn't like listening to a load of people talking about their problems. Going away feeling happy, not me, this type of talk depresses me. Well, I listened, and it just was not my bag, I knew I was in the wrong place. I am not knocking them; different things work for different people. I wanted to be back to my old self before bipolar. I wanted solutions and I wanted to find my way back.

Medically I was given tablets, I have been very shocked by the system in Ireland. I looked and asked questions and I asked for counselling, and it was not available to me. Even when your hospitalised you are not told anything about how to cope with your mental health, nothing. Your fed and watered and given a place to sleep. Your told nothing.

So fair enough you are going to have to sort this one out yourself. I just could not understand that these professional people had studied in a university mental health, but they explained nothing to you. In hindsight today I can see their Rational, but I do not think they are right. I was looking for answers and ways to help myself. I would love to know what they learnt in university.

After 10 years I demanded some help, eventually I was angry. I said to the psychiatrist "If this has taken me ten years to come to this point, I have learnt only what I have taught myself. Is it going to take me another 10 years to sort it out"? They allowed me to see a psychologist for 10 weeks, on the fourth week the girl said to me, she had been talking with her supervisor and they have decided that my sessions are finished. I agreed at the time because it was a real peeling of the onion situation, looking to the negatives.

I am extremely disappointed in the Irish system. Take your tablets and do the rest yourself and we will keep our knowledge to ourselves, come and tell me your problems. We will diagnose you Bipolar and not explain it to you. Now I find that crazy. Why? Do they want us to be sick forever, are we only numbers on a checque?

The things I learnt.

On to you, your journey is personal, your life is precious. I only know what I know through experience and through putting things into practice. Things I would like to share with you.

These are the things I needed to learn. To have gratitude for all that was in my life, I had to learn to love myself just as I am, I had to learn to accept my faults, I had to teach myself not to self-criticize, I needed to accept my life just as it is, I needed to learn to accept people as they are, I needed to learn how to let things go, I needed to teach myself how to look after myself, I needed to learn how to put myself first and I needed to grow up and be responsible for all of me and my life.

If I had not being Searching for answers, searching for my way out, searching for help, I think I would be still in that dark place and living a hopeless life.

Just taken tablets was not the answer.

So, here's what I have for you.

Bipolar
One foot in the right direction
My journey of discovery

- **Have you been diagnosed Bipolar?**
- **Would you like some help?**

- **Have you been struggling to come to terms with the situation you find yourself in?**
- **Have you been put on medication?**
- **Do you have regular visits to a doctor?**
- **What are your days like?**

Every person is an individual and every person's circumstances are not the same. The good news is that Bipolar's highs and lows can be quite similar, and we can change how we deal with our highs and lows. To find our middle ground.

It is particularly important that we learn to embrace our lives for all the good that is in them. Depending on where you are at, this can be quite hard to teach ourselves to be grateful for all that is good. When we find ourselves in a very dark place.

Give thanks all most like a mantra. This is to help you lift your spirits, you make yourself say Thank you for everything you can think of, like in my case.

Thank you for my home!
Thank you for my job!
Thank you for my health!
Thank you for my hands!
Thank you for my family!
Thank you for my friends!
Thank you for my feet!

The list goes on, everything you can think of. This really helps you lift your spirits. It lightens your day. Please give it a try and see for yourself how you feel. **Very important to check in with yourself notice how you feel.**

As a person who was dealing with bipolar, I could only deal with one task at a time and one day at a time. I got completely slowed down, this was both good and bad. Inside I did not want this, I wanted my old life back, but I could not reach this. I had to learn to take baby steps of improvements. A lot of the times I got stuck in depression, which I tried my best to hide,

I had negative feelings walking around with me, a sunken feeling and to be quite honest I found this life extremely hard to say the least.

Sometimes I would start to run, everything would seem like I was back to normal, the sunken feeling would leave, I would be on top of the world, I would be delighted. Everything would start to get easy. Before I would know it, I would be running around like a March hair, you name it, I would be up at the crack of dawn doing everything.

Not even realising I was in elation. I would not be able to bring myself back. (it's really for a comedy show) So once again I would end up in hospital.
This is the bones of what would happen to me, I was not able to control the Lows or the highs. I did learn I could live with depression but the elation I really needed to get a handle on it. Twenty years later I can write, it has been such a journey of self-discovery. I had to let go of all the fear I had about getting sick.

****

During a time of elation alarm bells need to be ringing very loud, to warn us to pay attention. If we catch it just as it starts, that is great because you can see what caused it. Sometimes only enjoying a good conversation can start elation, recognizing it, is the zone we need to be in but its more subtle and we do not always see it coming.

When I get creative, it has a way of starting that I don't see. With me its mixed in with getting excited about making something. I am aware of it, I take my tablets early, and I get away from people, the more energy I spend the stronger the elation gets.

What is the purpose of elation? As far as I can see, its purpose is to slow you down. It's there to warn you, that you are not in your reality of life, when you are in elation you are not on the same level as everyone else you are in your own zone and your feelings are elated too. If you don't stop, it moves on to the next level and that's Psychosis. You lose touch with reality, so you do get a chance to stop. If you don't stop there is always the next step.

Psychosis also needs to be recognized for what it is. When you notice your thoughts getting scrambled, things aren't real anymore. It's when your brain takes over and you have the strangest of experiences, you say the strangest of things, you do things you wouldn't normally do. If you notice this quickly and take your tablets go to bed and sleep, if you take control, it may pass. This is when doctors and hospitals are needed if you let it run free unattended.

I once had psychosis, I was put into hospital and I have absolutely no memory of what went on, for about 2 and a half weeks, this is so serious. People have killed in times of psychosis. You can see that when you have any of the early signs you have to act fast.

So please if you are experiencing elation, go home take your tablets, go to bed, sleep. It is a good idea to always carry a few tablets with you. As soon as elation starts take one. It will work straight away, and it will bring you down. The next step is so dangerous to you and to all around you.

I am writing this to try to help you." It is what it is", and it can change if you are willing to try.

In my times of psychosis, I did things that I got embarrassed of afterwards. To be embarrassed was a good thing, it made me be more careful, never to do the same thing again, so, all my stories are different, they are all really funny looking back. The madness belongs to me and nobody else. I did those crazy things. The embarrassment afterwards taught me lessons.

The journey is as hard as you make it, the power is within you. We share a similar chemical imbalance. What causes me to go out of sync could be different for you. Our journey will be different, hopefully the result will be the same.

A new way of dealing with life as it presents itself to you. Maybe you have already found some of the same answers as me, or you are looking for direction.

I knew after my second visit to a hospital because of elation turning into psychosis, (a three month stay). I knew I was doing something wrong, I needed to change. I was everyone's little helper, and I had put myself on the back burner so to speak. I knew this needed to change; I knew I was wrong.

Emotionally it was a rollercoaster ride, while I WOULDN'T change. Eventually the breaks were put on me. Bipolar was my breaks being pulled Tight. So, it was good, but it did not feel good at the time. I was in shock and Disbelief.

The first 10 years that I had bipolar disorder. I Struggled, my life had become an existence, when I would think I was getting things right. I'd go into elation. I must have been Hospitalized five times or more, I lost count. I also lost all my confidence and spontaneity for life.

The treatment in Germany for mental illness

Another time I took sick, too many things had happened all at once and I was in an elated state. I ended up going to Germany in that state, it very quickly got out of control, and I ended up in a German psychiatric hospital. The way they treated me was completely different to the care given in Ireland.

When I got there by ambulance, they brought me in and sat me down and gave me something to drink. They asked me no questions, they just said "drink this," it was to help me sleep, they showed me where I was to sleep handed me a fresh towel and showed me the bathroom where I could take a shower when I woke up, then told me to go to bed.

I went to bed and for three days solid I slept. My German friend Dani would ring every day, and they would tell her I was still sleeping. They said to Dani. "What the hell happened to that girl, that she needs that much sleep".

When I woke up, I felt normal, I had my shower in a private bathroom. They showed me where the common room was, where you could make tea any time you wanted. Fruit tea, it is the most common tea to drink in Germany. Outside the common room was a terrace with chairs and tables and a table tennis table if anyone wanted to play. They left me alone for a few days.

After a few days I was interviewed by three psychiatrists, they asked me about my madness. What was I thinking about at the time? I explained that I had been worried about one child, then my niece had taken tablets to kill herself, I was worried about her too, then the boy I had worked with for two years, had stabbed someone and the person was in a critical condition. On top of all that my sister had met a man from America on the internet and she invited him to stay in my house.

I knew I was in elation, but I needed to step back from the whole chain of events. "But what were you thinking"? I said that I started worrying about one child and ended up worrying about all the children in the world, one psychiatrist turned to the other and asked her. "About how many children were in the world". she said, "there are about 2 billion children in the world". Then he turned back to me and said, "Tell me Janet, how exactly where you are going to help 2 billion children". I shrugged my shoulders "I don't know". Knowing at the same time I could not help 2 billion children. This brang logic to my thinking.

One day they sent me for a body scan, little rubber pads were put all over me and a big machine recorded all the chemicals in my body. I suppose If I had of been taken drugs that would have shown up. They gave me a copy of it all.

The first few days I was in the observation unit, after that I was invited to join in the activities on their campus, it was a huge facility. These were all the therapies I took part in, art therapy, swimming therapy, dance therapy, sport therapy, music therapy and jewelry making therapy. These therapies made you realize that you needed to find time for you.

The meals were very good and balanced, you had to eat and put away your tray yourself, nobody picked up after you. We all got given times when we would have to keep the common kitchen tidy too.

In the campus there was a small supermarket, a church that did one Sunday service and a guest house where you could buy cake and coffee, beer and bar food or salad.

You didn't need to leave this place all your needs were seen to.

I was also given a video to watch on TV upstairs about Bipolar. It didn't work and that was a shame on my part. I handed it back and said nothing about it not working.

One day the doctors came to me extremely annoyed, holding my tablets. "Why are you on these tablets, these tablets are for epilepsy". I explained that in Ireland they are used as a mood stabilizer. She said, In Germany these drugs are for epilepsy, and we will not be returning them to you it is against German Law.

I had great treatment for two weeks in Germany, the best I had ever had. They made me own my madness, find time for myself, and they gave me dignity. Which is all missed in the Irish system from my personal perspective.

My normal stay in a hospital in Ireland would be three months, in Germany I was on my way home in two weeks. And back in work. I never told anyone in my Job I had just been in hospital only family and friends knew.

Back in Ireland

When I went to see the Irish psychiatrist, I told them I wanted to be kept on the tablets the German psychiatrist had subscribed. They wanted me back on a mood stabilizer tablet. I refused so the head consultant was called to the office. I explained the treatment I had received in Germany and how strange it was that I could be back and in work after two weeks, the mood stabilizer was not given to me.

In Germany even people that are not coping after a breakup, can end up in the same place I did, In Germany Depression is considered so serious that people are sent to a psychotherapist for two years, to help them get their lives back on track.

In Ireland I cannot paint the same picture. And it's shocking really.

But my visit to a German psychiatric Hospital really stood to me. I knew it was going to be up to me to get the help I needed.

I must explain my mood swings did not just happen like some people when they have bipolar. My mood swings happened when after an event, instead of getting angry I would internally mull over it, I'd end up in elation. So that's why today I don't want to care what anybody does anymore.

Learning Yoga

Christmas was an extremely hard time of year for me. So, one Christmas break I decided to go on a retreat. I ended up at the Burren Yoga Centre in Galway to do a Kundalini Yoga week. I turned a corner with everything, I learnt how to meditate, it was a real holistic approach. I came away with tools, I have been able to put into Practice ever since.

It is a place I always return to mostly at Christmas going into the new year. I was supposed to go this year but because of COVID-19 restrictions, it was canceled.

The Yoga teacher explained everything about the body and how everything works as one. He gave us so much information I was not able to take everything in but I learnt a lot. His Name is "Sotantar", and I will always be grateful for his Knowledge, his wisdom and his Light heartedness. I would have stayed; it was so good for me in every way. At that stage I had bipolar 10 years.

He explained how we can be enslaved by our thoughts, our brains always thinking. I knew exactly what he was saying to us. He told us, to pay attention to the thoughts in your head but only for a moment. Then let the thoughts go. He said, bring yourself to your breath, pay attention to the air as it enters your nose, follow that breath as it fills your lungs. He said this will bring you back to the present moment.

By regularly practicing this, every time your brain gets busy, it will always bring you back to the present moment. Also being aware of your other senses helps you to bring yourself to the present moment. That is where we are truly meant to be, that we are not meant to be living in our heads.

This was where I got one foot in the right direction. This was very Empowering. I was focused for some time after that. But I slipped back to being in a depressed state but at least I was able to meditate, this helped me lift my spirits.

A spiritual Healer

The one place that truly helped me, was a spiritual Healer and to this day from time to time I would visit this Lady, Margaret. I would go because of situations that were affecting me. Always my current situations. I would say that I was greatly affected by other people in my life, because I have never been a fighter, when I needed to give someone an answer, or just say "that wasn't very nice". I would go blank. So, I ended up mulling over the comments made by others, over and over in my head and attaching how these comments made me feel.

Margaret's insight and words of encouragement and her healings always helped me. I always walked away lifted and I would be able to cope. So, Margaret was my go-to women. I was skeptical about my first visit. I did not know how she worked but she helped me. I would go as far to say, I might not be here today if I had not met her.

Margaret has been a rock for me. She never judged, she understood, she cared, she often said to me you can just ring me, but I did not like to bother her unless I really needed help.

The answers did not come all at once, I had spent 14 years running around helping others and not myself. I was not living my true Authentic life. I didn't have the right Perspective on life. Margaret helped me Unravel the confusions I had caused. She'd bring logic to the table and help my understanding. Plus she helped me laugh at it all really.

The problem was me all the time, I was blocking my way. Yes, I was the last to find out, so it seemed. With Margaret's help, when I was down and not coping. I could go have a talk and have a healing and things kept moving along.

Eventually to a point where I put into practice what I was listening to. I did Rely on Margaret a lot through the years. As I progressed things got a lot easier. Margaret helped me to accept me, she helped me to be more grounded. When I had work trouble or a family crisis, I would nearly always end up going to Margaret.

Another healer I met truly helped.

During these years, I went all the way to Australia, to my brother Thomas's. (because I did not want to spend another summer on the couch). Every day he went to work, I got up and watched TV. Before he would come home, I would drive to the shops and buy dinner for him coming in from work.

He had given me a car to drive anywhere but I was so depressed, I just couldn't go or do anything. Thomas noticed my pattern. Every night when I cooked, I tried to hide my depression from him, but I went nowhere. Cutting the story short he found me out.

Because he cared he had a talk with me. He was right, I was stuck. He had never had a deep depression. I allowed him to give me his observations, but I was so stuck. All I could say to myself was Thomas doesn't understand depression, it has never been part of his life. I was wrong about that; he had experienced a person very close to him try to kill themselves and try to throw their life away.

I felt sad after his words because I always tried to function like everyone else and the depression was my secret, a very dark secret. I had truly very little will to live. I had lost my spirit for life. I just could not tell the people that I loved and my friends what exactly was going on within me. When I would be around other people, I was able to forget my depression a good bit and shelve it.

But when I was by myself the best thing, I could do was turn on the television and not think. Just getting out of bed in the morning was a hard chore for me. I would drag myself out of bed and go straight to the television, that was the type of energy I had for life.

After Thomas talked to me the next day I prayed to God. "God if this is really the level of life you want me to live, then OK ". My secret was out, Thomas knew I did nothing when I was by myself.

A funny thing happened, before I left for Australia my good friend Anna asked me. "Could you bring me back a Boomerang." Thomas was always working, I really needed to get the Boomerang for Anna. I could not go home without one. I wanted a real one, not the little ones in the airport that you hang on a wall.

Anyway, Thomas's friend and his girlfriend asked me out for lunch while Thomas was at work. We spent the day together, we went for a nice lunch, they were very kind to me, we went to the slot machines, they were so nice.

I never ask people to help me, I'm usually very independent, but I hadn't a clue where I'd get a real Boomerang. This was the most magical day, what happened next.

They took me to a real Authentic aboriginal gift shop; Michael Murphy was the owner. Upstairs in the gift shop Michael had an art studio, with lots of aboriginal pictures he had painted. They were interesting pictures, very much the same as Celtic art, completely different at the same time. He even had didgeridoos, and he played one for us, it had a very hunting mystical natural sound, a kind of groaning.

So, I started looking at all the paintings, I left everyone talking to themselves. At one stage, there was only Michael and me upstairs. I shared with him that I also painted, I explained that my pictures were all from my imagination, that the funny thing was. I would start a painting with an idea in my mind, when I would finish the painting, it would be different to what I had seen in my mind. I said, "painting is like a journey".

He said to me that is not the way a painting in your mind should be. That when you have a picture in your mind to paint, the picture should turn out exactly as you have seen it in your mind. He said I was under a spiritual attack, he said he was a spiritual healer.

I paused for a moment when he said that, inside my head, I heard, "ask him for a healing, ask him for a healing." So, I said, "I have depression, could I pay you for a healing". He said "No", a blunt No, then he said. "If I was to take money from you, I'd lose the gift I have." Inside my head, quick ask him again, don't mention money. So, I asked him again, very humbly, I said, "could you do a healing for me". He took a deep look at me.

He explained how a dark spirit had come into my life when. It was not allowing me to have what I wanted in life, even when I painted. As soon as he talked to me, tears were rolling and rolling down my face. He said that when I was a child someone with a dark spirit had come into my life. He said that I had taken some of their ways, that was why the dark spirit was able to come into my life.

He drew on a piece of paper how I was, and he also drew how I was meant to be, it was in a picture form very easy to see, he said this is how you are, but this is how you are meant to be, he said you are never to accept being like (the first picture). You are always to be like the second picture. You have a beautiful spirit, and you are meant to shine so brightly. You were so bright that is why the dark spirit was attracted to you so much.

He gave me an ostrich feather for protection. He also told me that I needed to burn all my clothes. That I was to get an earthenware pot and a black pen and write all the things "Tommy" had taken away from my life on the pot. I was then to break the pot and scatter the pieces in all different directions.

Then when we were back downstairs in his shop, he gave me two things, a pen and a notebook, he told me I would write when I'm ready, that I would travel a lot. I will always remember the smiles he gave me, his eyes mouth and his whole face smiled. It was beautiful.

I bought a lovely Boomerang and a few bits for friends back home and we went, when we got into the car, I was overwhelmed by what had just happened, surprised indeed, something had shifted.

The next day when I sat at the side of the bed, I was giddy. It was a new experience. I went to a garden center and bought an earthenware pot, I headed for the beach. With all the new clothes I had bought, I burned them. I had to go very far down the beach to do this because you're not allowed burn in Australia, but I did. Then I put what was left in a bin. I set on the beach with the Pot, my black pen and I wrote all the things I could remember. The pot was full of writing even on the inside. You wouldn't think one dominant person could do so much. I had to leave the beach to break the pot, it wouldn't break in the sand.

I went to the bus stop, I broke it, picked up all the pieces, put some in the bin, threw some in the bushes and walked back to the shoreline. As I walked along one by one, I threw each piece in the sea, the very last piece I had in my hand. I decided to look at it and you know what was written on it "Tommy." I got it and with true conviction I threw it in the sea.

A few days later I returned to the shop to thank Michael because I was in such a good place. I baked him and his wife a cake. He gave me some more advice. This I am sharing with you because this advice ended up been the main tool that I have used to get over Depression, dark feelings and self-criticism. I have been sharing it with anyone that needed it because it really works.

I had a friend Paddy in my car one evening, we were going to a Kundalini yoga class, he told me he had suicidal thoughts. I did not know what to say to him. On our journey back I had an ah ha moment. I touched his knee and said "I know what I need to tell you, I need to tell you what the aboriginal man told me. I told him what I'm about to tell you, about three weeks later I asked him how he got on. He smiled and told me it worked for him. To this day he uses the same practice. Me too.

Michael said when the dark feeling comes again, just stop what you're doing. Do not think any thoughts, don't look, don't move, don't ask any questions. Do this for a moment and it will go away. He said it will try to come again, do the same thing and it will go. After you do this for a moment just go and do something like make a cup of tea and you will notice the shift. This really works, please give it a try. He also said if you do this the dark spirit will leave you alone.

It was the truth what Michael told me about my past. I had taken some of the ways of Tommy. When I was handling arguments within my marriage. I would go to Tommy, and he would give me advice, I would then do what he said to do and when something needed to get sorted. I would say to myself "What would Tommy do"? I would keep the argument up till I got my way. So, I did open myself up to that spirit.

By doing what Michael told me I was able to get rid of the dark feelings of depression, control bad feelings and stop self-criticizing

It also taught me that you were to handle your life yourself and not look to other people for their input, that we are to find our own way in life.

A lot of young copy their mother's and father's. Tommy was not my father; he was a dominant person, and everything changed in our house to his ways, even how my mother made stew. I would have been Ok with Tommy had he not been violent. A lot of men were bossy in those days. He always criticized and found fault with everything and everyone.

My understanding on depression

Depression as you know is a very dark place and It's very hard to pull away from it. Really, it's a bad feeling, a sunken feeling, it does come and go. When it comes it actually debilitates you, it stops you living your correct life, selfcare goes out the window. Not washing, not eating, not cleaning. I didn't self-harm, but some people do, but I did self-sabotage, and I kept myself in that cycle.

Feelings are not real, action is real. So first I'd have a thought, I might want to do something, like have a shower, then I get a sunken feeling or a thought that would say, no not now. I'd stay watching TV and the shower wouldn't happen till the weekend was over, I'd really have to push myself. The funny thing was that when I'd have that shower, I'd feel great, I'd look great, and my mood would lift.

What people said and did, depending on how close they were to me, would affect me. I have always been the type of person that froze and never had the right thing to say back to someone. I might have the words two days later, but it would be too late, so this is how I'd be hurt because I didn't stand up for myself. Basically, I was so governed by my feelings I allowed all things to bother me.

My mother would not really agree with what I just said there, because with the people I am close to I can stand my ground, I just don't argue about every little thing, only when something is very important. I do stand my ground, and we shout at each other.

I comfort ate.

After something happened, I would come home from work with about three boxes of cakes, "Hi Anna I just got these for us". I put them in the corner in the kitchen. Anna's first words one day to me were." What happened in work today?" I paused. "Well actually, something did happen in work today." I lived with Anna for two years, she seen my pattern, I comfort ate, I did this for years, it was pointed out for me. This really helped me to look and see it for myself.

I was then able to see it for myself, I realized, maybe it has something to do with the inner child. When I was a child, if I hurt my knee, my granny put me on her knee, she hugged me when I was crying and sent me to the shops to buy two Pink Panther bars, they were my favorite and she knew it. One was for me and the other was for her.

She knew if she distracted me with sweets I'd stop crying.

So, I looked at the situation me bringing home cakes, Anna was right.

When you see something for what it is, it can change.

Allowing everyone their space to be as they are

I have had to come to a point in my life now, that I don't care what anyone says or does, it's not my business, and I'm teaching myself not to be shocked, people say and do bitchy things. I don't care, they can do what they want, I let a lot go over my head. It is not my business. My Mother can now say what she wants, I don't care, and I am able to move past a lot. I won't take my eye off that ball ever again, when it gets thrown in my direction, I'm not playing anymore, the game is off the cards. I really do hope I will live up to every word I have just written.

Every person can live say and do whatever they want to. My opinions only work for me in my life. That is how it is to stay.

Did you ever hear someone say just before a fight? "Who asked you for your opinion, why are you butting in here, nobody asked you your opinion, get the …. k away, mind your own business." I've heard that, and they are 100% correct. Another good one is "keep your opinions to yourself, nobody wants to hear your opinions."

I have been a very opinionated person, I liked other people's opinions, but I liked mine the best, do you want to know the big Joke, my opinions came from other people and the conditioning of the times I lived. Sure, I had a different opinion, but secretly I had heard someone else say them first. That is so funny today really.

Put yourself First in your life and do the things you want to do.
Do you love yourself. Have you allowed yourself to love yourself?
Well, I thought I did because of my ego and my vanity, what does Love look like in your life?

To love yourself you have to be responsible for all your needs, I love myself means, I will care for myself, sometimes we don't understand. We see love from a family point of view, and we keep doing for others and not for ourselves. I had to think about that a lot. I had to get myself out of other people's business and into my own business.

Can you hear yourself saying I want my old life back? Well as soon as you start looking after your needs, you will get it all back, but it starts with you first. Give yourself time for you.

When I had a family problem recently, I just kept saying to myself "**it is what it is**". These five little words helped me to see realistically. I really didn't want the problem, and it took me some time to realize that I didn't want it at all. I did feel compelled to do something to offer some help, I said at the time if it knocks on my door, I will help, but I really needed to hold myself back, and I did for weeks, eventually I said I'm going to have to say "No". I really didn't want anyone else's problems; I could only see disaster if I helped.

Why did I jump in so fast? Because I thought, I knew best.?????
Why did my family allow me to, and not shut me down? because it suited them.

No regrets, anything I did in the past was to help and not hinder. The problem with it all for me was, that I had squeezed myself out of my life, and ended up mentally unwell.

Well, that's all changing, and I'm stepping back. Everyone is doing it for themselves now. It took time to change, you want to know what the joke is, if you don't help someone, they do help themselves. It was only me that needed to change. That is so funny when I think back. It's really funny today.

How did I change, what is self-love and how important is it in our lives? It is everything and it gives you back your life? Putting yourself first is not a selfish act, it is the correct thing to do, and it comes down to all the basic ways of living. Things everyone in the world does, except all the depressed people. If we don't say it as it is, we will continue in that cycle. I had to grow up, saying No is necessary sometimes.

Fear

I was always afraid of life, things that might go wrong, making a mistake, saying the wrong words. So, I hid myself in all those fears. I created a personality that could hide in those fears. I did everything as correct as possible as to not make a mistake in life. The problem with that is that I lived to other people's standards, not to my own and I wanted my family to live to my standards too, Janet knows best. I had a lot to learn because I had set myself up for a big fall.

I heard this along the way somewhere, and I agreed with it. Your parents do their best as they are rearing you, and they provide all that they can, but when you become an adult, you have to give yourself all that you need. Your parents' job is finished. I totally agree with this, but I did not realize it was also talking about self-love, nobody can give that to you, you have to give it to yourself.

The promises I made to myself.

It all came down to me making promises to myself that were realistic, considerably basic promises, I had to start with one thing at a time. When I tried to do everything all at once, after a day or two I would be back to my old tricks sitting around doing nothing. Not cooking my dinner, doing nothing. I was like a baby crawling for the first time.

I knew I needed a new approach, so I thought to myself, what if I always had dinner. I promised myself that I would not skip dinner, so I started having dinner every day. I did not care if it was out of a chipper or the Chinese, I was having dinner, I didn't care if it was two fried eggs, if I called It dinner, it was my dinner. I was still lying on the couch and the dishes sometimes were not washed for a few days, but I was having dinner.

I then moved on to breakfast, If I bought everything, I needed for breakfast I could have breakfast every day. This consisted for me of coffee, milk, bread, Jam, eggs, yogurt and porridge. I always had breakfast at the weekends, but during the week it was a real hit and miss situation, so I started to bring yogurt with me to work or an apple, once I ate something, I was happy.

So, dinner and breakfast were solved but I was still lying on the couch watching TV. I made another plan. I told myself before I'd go to bed, I'd wash the dishes every night and I stuck to that, and this worked too. Every one of these things only stayed because I did them one by one. This way really worked for me, it could work for you too.

These are all very basic things, things that people do automatically, I know you Know as I do that, they can all fly out the window when you have a depression. In my case the depression was gone at this stage, but my mojo was not there anymore. I had taught myself lots of very bad habits. So, I had to take baby steps and be pleased with each one before this body would trust me again. Mojo, enthusiasm or spirit for life. Why would it trust coming back to a woman still lying around?

Why was I still finding it hard to clean my house, why was I still lying on the couch watching TV, in all my spare minutes? Mojo did not come back till I was so sick of it all.

This really helped me get enthusiastic about life.

I got an idea, what if I asked my niece Leanne, could her daughter Alannah come to my house Saturday mornings. I would pay her 10 euros an hour and if she helped me, she'd be happy and I would too, I said to Leanne, I don't really need her to clean much, but I need the enthusiasm that a child has to get that money to be with me while I cleaned.

Leanna thought it was a great Idea and she thought Alannah would love to do that. Cutting the story, I cleaned, and Alannah tidied a draw and then she tidied another draw, and I cleaned the rest of my house myself. Another time she came, and we baked, I benefited from her just been there, and we have a weekly arrangement, she comes for two hours, she gets 20 euro, I have the house clean before she comes, I stay on top of it all, and she comes to help. It was the cry for help that I needed, she might go out for a walk or go shopping with me. Think about it I needed help. I thought of a solution, it worked. It is now 2024 Alannah is getting on with her own life now but her helping me was a great start.

If you ask yourself questions you will find answers.
Depression as I see it.

What is depression, is it a bad feeling, how can it be so debilitating, how can it have such power in our lives????

If you do not learn how to get rid of depression it's going to stay as long as you allow it, what is its function?

Depression is there to wake you up, yes, it's there to make you appreciate the life that you have but the deeper you go into it, the deeper the bad thoughts can be, the more debilitating it can be on you and your life. You lose your direction, you lose your future, you lose your days. Is it real, yes, it is, it can also kill? Can it go, YES?

Are you guilty like me of holding on to the past, I know the past may have hurt us all, but the past is not your problem today, it's depression? Your depression is a result but it's here to teach you something about yourself. Its job is to make you go in a new direction, in the past I was facing the wrong way, I thought so little of myself.

You may be like me have wanted your old life back, but when you get rid of depression you get a chance of a new life. Same house, same street, same job, same friends, same family, same you, same nature and same faults. A whole new experience because nothing in your life needs to change.

When you get the chance to have life again you walk very carefully, it started for me with baby steps. It's like you're on the right path, there is really nothing wrong with you, but your head is pointed in the wrong direction, and you need it to turn and face the other way, live in your present moments, facing the Beauty and wonder of what's to come.

If having depression can bring death. Looking the other way, everything has two sides, the opposite of depression is life, it really is, and it is the one thing we really want.
But we do need help. You have the answers to your needs. So, find your way.

Is depression a good thing, not when you're in the middle of it, but when you learn how to take control of it. **When it comes, Stop, pay attention, give a moment and allow it to pass**, it passes. If you do not do that you can have a bad day, acceptance of everything is a golden Key.

These things happen, you can say, "I don't like what he just said." He said it. You didn't. He can keep it. I do not care. I am not catching that ball. It is what it is, people say things. This will help you not take things on board. Take nothing from nobody, it's all a big game and learning to dance, jump, smile, move away if you have to.

When we are drumming to someone else's beat, how can we beat our own beat, learn to beat your own drum, make your own cake, dance your own dance, depression is here to stay if we don't find our own way in life. Our friends and family are only waiting to see us shine once more.

Holding on to Feelings stops the flow of life.

Feelings come and go, if we choose to hold on to them, we attach our feelings to our memories, so when we think of a memory, we relive that anger again. If we think of it again, we get angry again. This is a crazy cycle of life. Why does that happen. It's actually a very clever part of our existence.

Have you ever heard someone say, "I don't want to talk about that, that makes me feel bad? "or "I get angry every time I think of that". There is a lesson in that for us all, we are not meant to think about the past in that way. When we have Hindsight, we can look and laugh because we can then see the mistakes that belong to ourselves in it all, and then we find clarity.

Even right now me writing and you reading is not all the answers. We never have all the answers, we never know the story from the other persons perspective. We only know things from a one-sided angle. You can never look around a corner and see what's there till you actually go to the corner and take a look for yourself. Its ok for me to tell some of my story but if I told the full story I would relive those feelings.

If you wake up feeling down, recognize the feeling. Say, "I am feeling down, "Freeze your thoughts, do not think anything for a moment, don't move one finger or one hair on your head, sit still for a moment and by doing this the feeling can pass by. Do this every time you have a sunken feeling after a moment, go do something (make yourself a Cup of tea).

And when your lying-in bed not getting up because you're thinking. Realize you are spending your time thinking, stop for a moment, look at the wall, the thinking will stop because you are looking at the wall, and as soon as you can, jump out of

that bed before another load of time-wasting thoughts, jump into your head and try to rob your day.

It's only a matter of putting this into practice. You will get good results. **Giving yourself space between your feelings is so special, it is a golden key that will help you.**

Feelings are funny, Love hate, Joy pain, there are two sides, and we have choices to make. I choose to live a happy content life, I choose to appreciate my days as they unfold, I choose to be responsible, and I choose to be kind and caring to myself.

We need our feelings, to feel love, to feel Joy, to feel happy, to feel sad, to feel pain but do we really need to be sad, every day. This is an emotional roller coaster ride that we have ourselves on, it all depends on how we are treated that will determine how we feel. And the Joke is that if we meet our personal needs, we get stronger and we learn to depend on ourselves for our needs, we learn that we are important to ourselves and we will look after ourselves in a good way.

We are all beautiful people and just living a life is so important, you are so important. We are all here to shine as bright beings. Each new day has new possibilities.

Understanding and logic

I really feel we are here to learn. People that do not have depression do not fully understand how could they. I do not know what it's like to be a bus driver, only a fellow bus driver knows the full story. The same is true for depression, before I got it, I really didn't know what it was going to be like, and with having Bipolar, because it goes from depression to Elation, you're not always depressed and you get fooled thinking it's gone, then it comes back like a big bang. That is why I call it a roller coaster ride. Both sides of It can be extremely dangerous, Detrimental.

I had lost my way for such a long time, that even when I got a handle on depression, I had picked up bad habits, these bad habits made it look like I was still in depression, and I knew I was not. It did eventually make me ask the question or say. OK Janet, the depressed feelings are gone and if they come again, you know what to do. Why can't I clean my house, why can't I clean me, why can't I feed me.???

Really look at yourself, do you have food, do you have shelter, do you have friends, do you have family. Look at all that is around you. Years ago, people would say, "take stock of what you have." That is so needed here. If you do not do that, see what you do have, you will be making excuses for yourself. Bipolar can just stay where it is. Labels belong on Jam jars not on people.

1. You are not what you think.
2. Life is not what you think.
3. Your thoughts can be controlled by you.

We do need to listen to what our heads are saying to us, but we are not to believe those thoughts. We need to say back to the thought stop, no, we have negative thoughts we have creative thoughts both need to be controlled if you are bipolar.

Here is a simple example, but one that taught me so much.

I have a key ring with many keys, when I put the wrong key in the shed door, my head would say, "you're a stupid bitch," "you fool." Mostly I'd call myself "stupid." This is not good, it is so subtle, it's only a small sunken feeling and it passes because I choose the correct key, but this is where the lesson is.

I decided the next time I put the key in the shed door, if I choose the wrong key, I am not going to call myself "stupid". So, I put that into practice. The next time I needed to go into the shed. I put the wrong key in the door again but this time I said nothing, I got the correct key put it in the door and I did not call myself stupid.

When you insult yourself, believe it or not your whole being does not like that, how I know this, I stopped calling myself stupid and my mind started letting me laugh when things happened. So, for the best part of my life, I did this. For years, but as soon as I said I'm not doing that anymore my mind played ball, my mouth stopped saying it, and I had lots of happier experiences, this is the truth the whole truth and it's amazing.

Try it if you self-Criticize. You must become your best friend. You wouldn't criticize someone else for making a mistake, you'd probably laugh, you have to do the same with yourself, Laugh.

I told a friend of mine what I did with the key's, he very cleverly said. Why don't you put a bit of tape on the correct key, and you won't call yourself stupid…?

Ah ha. I'm enjoying at the moment not calling myself stupid, many things have happened, that I didn't call myself stupid, to the point were. One time recently I belly laughed all by myself when I came home from the shops with two lightbulbs, from two different shops, on the same day, for the light in the sitting room…you have to laugh, it was great. A real belly laugh. I had forgotten while I was shopping that I had already got the lightbulb in the first shop.

Something we don't always understand. It is so important to learn to love yourself. Have a talk with yourself and promise yourself that you will care about all your needs.

Another Journey I took was, I joined the Christian Fellowship.

This is a Christian Church, I stopped being a Catholic because I never agreed with everything they did. I came away from the catholic idea because I only believed in Jesus and God, all the rest I didn't believe.

After a few years I joined up with the Christians, the reason I joined was they believed in Jesus and God, and they studied the bible. This I agreed with at the time, and the people I met were lovely. That lasted for three years, and I learnt a lot about myself and the Bible. But I reached a stumbling block. I pulled away from the group. I decided to keep my faith with God my own business.

Having faith really helped me in my darkest hours, I called on God for help, I can say that faith has been the one thing that has really kept me together. But you must help yourself too.

I did learn that we need to forgive everyone, if you forgive everyone, it really helps you to drop any anger and hurt you may still be carrying around with you. We all make mistakes, say the wrong things, hurt someone. So, by forgiven others we can also forgive ourselves. Every one of us has faults, faults we cannot see. I did return to the Christian church because it is something I want and need at this moment in my life, and I think I'll be a Christian forever, but I only know life to this moment.

Feelings are not you.

You can be controlled by your feelings, are you either up or down, are you ok when you are around others, not ok when you are by yourself. Why can't you stay in the middle.?
Holding a door at a shop for somebody that is rude, they expect you to hold the door for them. You're sorry you held the door because of their arrogance. They didn't deserve your kindness.

That situation and those sunken feelings you forget quite quickly. You move on past the door, you look at something new, you lose the feelings because this person is not important enough to worry about or bring you down. Hello, it's just a passing situation. They didn't deserve your kindness; we mark it up as "I won't be in a hurry to hold a door again" We get over it.

Yet if someone we love hurts our feeling's we remember it again and again and we relive the memory with the same feelings and drag ourselves down. We attach our memories with the feelings. That's all quite normal.

We really need to let the past sit in the past, not bring it into our present moments. There is nothing really in it that we can change today, so we need to just let it go. It serves no purpose in your life today.

You may be saying if that had not happened, I wouldn't be here today. My stance on that type of thinking is that as we journey through our life, we are doing our best all the time. Things may have happened and at the time I coped with them the best way I knew then, let it all go, be present with your current situation, and seek help if you're not coping today.

How do we stop this emotional rollercoaster ride?
How can we control our feelings.?

41

Feelings change all the time; we need to learn a new way of dealing with them. Before we can understand this, we need to look at it with a clear Perspective.

First comes Thought.
Second comes Feelings.
Third comes Action.

You are the only person that can control your feelings, first you must listen to the thoughts in your head, is your mind randomly racing one thought after another. Your head can keep you from action. You might want to do something, and your mind says not now, it's mind control but it's not the true sense of the mind, the mind will keep you busy all the time. When you get control of your thinking your mind goes silent.

You notice the thought it might be a negative thought or a creative thought, but it's only a thought so let it go.

Just like when you held the door for someone rude. When you moved away from that door to something new, you forgot about your feelings, the memory stayed only a memory without feelings, you didn't really relive the feelings. Feelings can come and go if you choose. If you choose to hold on to them, they stay as long as you want them to. Yes, it is by choice.

It is so important to get control over your Thoughts and your feelings. In depression they have taken control of your mornings, your days and your years. One by one they can add up to a tidy sum.

Your life is Precious, and your days are numbered, and they belong to you alone. Nobody is responsible for you, you are so special and there's a reason you are on this journey with Bipolar, you must learn to take back the rains of your existence. Learn to be a driver once again. Drive your life for you, for the first time really.

If you choose to see feelings just like the wind blowing your hair, when the wind stops your hair settles. We need our feelings to feel love, to feel joy, to feel happy, to feel sad, but do we really need to feel sad every day, so we need to address this, it is an emotional rollercoaster ride, one that you and I have the power to stop.

Have you ever had a situation where you decided to let go over your head, you did nothing, you didn't voice your opinion, you just didn't get involved, you just let the hair sit and to your surprise you were able to step right back from the whole situation? Well, it is the same with your feelings, feeling down feeling annoyed, feeling frustrated, feeling angry?

I had a regular problem that would happen to me, sometimes like a wave of resentment or anger, a really bad feeling would come over me, this only happened with people I was close to.

One day I was washing the dishes after lunch and this wave came over me, a ratty feeling, I had a talk with myself. Seve, my good friend from Spain was visiting for two months.

Anyway, I recognized the feeling, I said Janet if you say nothing, he has no way of knowing you're in a bad mood, then I remembered what the aborigine man Michael told me to do for a dark spirit, so I put it into practice. I stopped what I was doing, thought nothing, didn't move, didn't think, paused for a moment. Then I started washing the dishes again, the Ratty, angry feeling was gone.

This is very important, I had had those types of feelings, since I was young and they would stay with me for days, and I would not be happy till it would turn into a fight.

I had thought myself how to control it, and now it's gone. If it comes again, I know what works.

If you came to a moment when you feel any of these feelings, recognize the feeling, it is usually a bad feeling, a sunken feeling, an irritated feeling. First recognize the feeling, do not reach, or respond, freeze all thoughts, freeze all movements. Just do this for a moment after you have done this, then just go and do what you need to do. Go make a Cup of tea.

This space you give yourself between your feelings is so special, a Golden tool, that will help you in every situation, if you do this you will be able to take control of your days. And your feelings will not control you anymore.

We are all beautiful people, we are all here to shine as bright beings, each day is a new day. What happened yesterday is over and done with, sit in your situation. Know what is good for you. This is back to giving thanks. Really look, do you have food, do you have shelter, do you have friends, do you have family. Look at all that is around you.

Sometimes we are so in our minds that we don't really appreciate what is around us, we allow our past to dictate our days and our future thoughts, so as to Rob us of the true realities. Consuming our days in a very negative manner, bringing all of our days into one and when this happens to us, we experience life mundanely, hopelessly.

Eventually I felt robbed this had taken too many of my years. I would never have gotten better If I had not started to care about my basic needs. You have to know what you want and don't want; you have to become your own help; I could go different places for help.

In the simple things that I did and the promises I made to myself. I have given myself back my life.

Structure to my day, things that I now do automatically. I now want to look after myself, I now want to live each day. I now want to be my best friend.

When you make a promise to yourself. Do not make it so big, just do the little things that you know you could do. Start with one when you know its mastered think of another and in this way, you will get your strength back and you will be the one sitting in the driving seat.

There are no regrets for the past, you were only doing what you thought was best at the time. Hindsight is great but nobody has it, if I only knew then, what I know now, I would have done things differently. Yes, we all say that what I love about all that is, when you get clarity It's all so funny really. It was all part of your journey to bring you to today.

Your mindset and how you see life really will determine how your days go. Start listening to your thoughts, are they negative, tell them to stop.

When I'm driving my car sometimes my head would say "you're going to have a crash". It's just a negative thought trying to come in. I tell it to go away, I don't believe a word. I do this with all negative thoughts. You do have to pay attention. If I don't do that, they know they can stay.

Voices in my head

I also experienced a voice in my head. My Grandmother had died. The first night I was in my own bed again, I lay down and I heard an audible voice in my head say, "Your Next." I was happy because I was in the middle of my depression and also in grief. I would not mind dying, but it was a real voice. I allowed that voice into my life that night.

On and off for the next two years something would happen, and the voice would come again. It always had the same message "Your Next". I had no control over it, it would just randomly happen. I told no one.

One night my two friends were staying over. I was taking them to the airport at 5am. Just before I fell asleep the voice came. "You're going to have a car crash." I said back to the voice. "No. Anna and Val will be in the car".

Then my mind showed me a picture of the crash, with the car pointing at the return journey from the airport. It showed me the bonnet of the car all crumpled and the dashboard. I had an **AH ha!** Moment, I said back to the voice and the picture in my mind. "You've never shown me a picture before, will you ever go and F…k off, and leave me alone". I said nothing to Anna or Val, but after I dropped them to the airport, on the journey where the crash was going to happen, there was no crash.

This thought me that the mind could play tricks on you. You're not to believe it. The voice continued to come, each time after that I would tell it to go, I never believed it again. The voice got quieter and quieter, and I could even hear it like a very little man, saying "Your next". I said to that little voice to go away too. That was the last time I heard a voice. It took about two years to get rid of the voice, so all these things take time, and you must stay focused.

12-12-21
Janet ♡

47

The voice did stop but I noticed that the voice and the negative thoughts were the same in some way, they would come, and I'd tell them to go as well. This all worked well for me, so well that my head was clear a lot of the time.

So please do not believe any voices or thoughts in your head, anything in your head is a lie.

If you ask a question an answer will come, and it's generally good. So, don't be happy with your situation, do ask for help, do ask yourself questions. Maybe if I had been more honest about depression the road would not have been so long. But it was what it was for me.

Take a piece of paper and write down all your good points. You will be surprised how many good points you truly have; this is a particularly good exercise.

Pay attention to the things you say, learn to be your best friend. Mentally we can be against ourselves, its only by paying attention that we can catch ourselves doing this.

I had a lot of work to do to get myself right but as soon as I started putting things into practice like, not calling myself stupid, I was on the road to success. As I started caring for myself and all my needs, I got stronger. Asking for a little help from Alannah has also helped me keep order.

I do have bipolar disorder, and I take my medication every night. I live one day at a time. Yesterday has very little interest to me and the future is looking after itself. Being present is my whole interest and being responsible for myself is my concern. I've had to show myself compassion for all what I put myself through, it's really great because it helped me to change my ideas on what's important in life.

I didn't say much about elation, when I have elation. I have to act fast, recognize it, take a tablet early, calm down, slow down, stop and sleep. When I started writing this book, I was so excited that the elation was able to sneak in and I didn't notice it.

When I started to get scrambled thoughts, my head was telling me, "This wasn't the truth" I realized after the third thought, what my mind was doing. I went straight to the press, took out my tablets and took two sleeping tablets along with my other tablets and I went straight to bed. For me Elation is there to tell you to stop. **SO, STOP YOU HAVE GONE TOO FAR.**

This is the only stance I have on elation, I am not afraid of it anymore because I am in control and I know, If I take my tablets early it settles right down. If that doesn't work for you go straight to your doctor and tell him he will help you.

Bipolar how I came to this point

I have a story that happened while I was living at Anna's, we were all going for a little Christmas break to a nice hotel in Wicklow. We were all starting from Anna's house because she was making one of her breakfast fries. Anna, Val, Sarah, Paddy and the two grandchildren Aaron and Emily and myself. We were all sitting around the table Anna was at the cooker getting everything ready.

I was elated, Paddy was smiling at what I had just said, Anna and Val were not happy with me, they knew I was in elation, they were ignoring me. So, I knew I was upsetting them, because I don't like to upset people, I said to myself I should just go up to my room and take one table, this was the first time I had ever one of my tablets in the daytime. Before we left Anna's house I calmed down, the elation stopped, it's quieted me down.

When we got to the hotel, we went into our rooms, I went into mine and I slept till the next day. The elation was no longer there.

So, after that Christmas when I went back to work, I brought some tablets with me, one day I was in elation in work I went to my locker, and I took half a tablet, and this worked too, on my next visit to the psychiatrist, I told him what I did that worked. On the second visit to the psychiatrist, I went to him to ask if he could give me a smaller tablet to carry with me to help me control the elation. He had already decided that they would give me a small tablet of 25gm and if it happens, I could take up to two tablets along with my medication. This really worked for me.

Another thing happened to me a long time after, one day I was in work and I had a very nice conversation with a new colleague, a very nice person. One of the first things she said to me was that she had depression, so I automatically wanted to help her with what I knew might help her. For about 10 minutes I spoke with her and in the end she took the number of my friend Margaret because I told her Margaret had helped me. When I went into the next room to do my work, I realized I was elated just because I had a conversation. I calmed myself down and didn't talk to anyone, I noticed the elation energy in my body, it was like I just paused relaxed, and it didn't take flight, it stopped. This was a new experience. I learnt that if you notice the elation right as it starts and relax and give it none of you are taught and don't panic it can stop quickly and not take hold.

I did get sick again unfortunately but this time I had come off my medication, ego basically, I was doing really well so I decided to try life without medication and say nothing to nobody, I was good for a few months it was April I lasted till June. I ended up in Blanchardstown hospital, their treatment there is different, only they have men and women sleeping together and I nearly got raped by a very sick man. I got moved to another ward. Two days later another young girl was raped by the same man. I had seen the man staring at me intensely I got frightened, but he kept staring. He made me panic, I warned the nurses, they seemed to think it was just my bipolar and it wasn't. that poor girl. He got sent to another hospital Dundrum.

They changed my medication, and they took me off the tablets that I got given in Germany and they stopped given me the little tablet that helps me when I'm elated.

Last summer they gave me back the little tablet to control elation as it starts. So, I have been coping well.

I recently had a very strong elation, I've had to add this into the writings because it was not my normal elation and it didn't act in the normal manner and even when I took my tablets and went to bed, I was still in elation.

I taught this book was completed; I needed feedback from my friend Anna she has read more books then you could imagine, I needed some approval you see English is my weakest area so my grammar isn't that good.

All around me there was good news, my Niece got a house off a housing agency. She had been waiting more than twelve years to get housed. Sarah Anna's daughter had been made permanent in her job in Tallagh hospital, My Sister is happy in the hostel she is in, waiting to be housed and her children are happy there too, Dean my nephew has a little girl friend, Cassie my niece has got her figure back and the weight has gone, Emily Sarah's daughter was accepted to play with Shelburne park, Arron Sarah's son was accepted onto a level 6 sports course which leads on to college and I had completed my story.

So, all around me was good news, I was excited about all the good news, two separate families. Connected because they are cousins really.

I think my ego had a role to play, I was so excited about finishing my story and my best friend Anna liked It.

Today I had a visit with the psychiatrist, and I had to tell him what I had done wrong and what had caused this elation, that I was elated since Saturday. Last Friday night I had a drink in my friend's house, So, We had a drink we danced to a song or two and we had a laugh well I wasn't laughing when I realized I had forgotten my tablets.

I only drink Martini, it's not strong and I don't drink much. But I knew I wouldn't sleep without my tablets. We went to bed I could not sleep; I gave up trying and it was four a.m. I came downstairs and I typed. And smoked my last two cigarettes. Around six a.m. I went back to bed I hoped I'd sleep, I couldn't so I just rested.

I went into a high elation, and I could not stop talking and telling funny stories. The next morning, I was in elation and Sarah, and I laughed and laughed and when a good song came on the radio, we got up from the breakfast table and we jumped around, you know that song, "Jump Around", we were enjoying the morning. Instead of going for a walk I suggested doing the garden work, and we got Sarah's Garden ready for the summer.

She listened to all my funny stories, anyway it felt like it was seven in the evening, when I got into my car, I asked Sarah the time and it was only two. We both looked at each other and laughed. I had talked so much it felt like hours had gone by.

I went straight home I knew the next step is psychosis so as soon as I got in, I took my medication and two sleeping tablets, I went straight to bed till six the next morning. I had fifteen hours of sleep. Normally the elation goes away at that point, but it didn't.

Yesterday Monday I was still elated right from the get-go. I'm cutting this story because It's getting too long to get to the point I want to. Monday I was sent home from work, and it was suggested to me to go see my doctor, I agreed, and I got an appointment for today. I also got time off till next Monday.

I told the psychiatrist everything, the book, the cover letter, the people that helped me. I said that I don't go into depression anymore, but I keep going into elation. For the last two months or so since December. I have been in and out of elation when the depression has come and it did try last week, I just stamped one foot on the ground and said No and I jumped up and down this helps you ground yourself. And it went straight away.

I asked the psychiatrist does he knew anyway how to get rid of elation because I have also been handling elation easier than this weekend. Normally I'd take my tablets early and go to bed and it would be gone. This was the first time it didn't work for me, and I am now in elation since Friday, it has not really stopped.

Today the psychiatrist told me things I had never heard before, and I spoke to him with anger that I have about the system here dealing with my mental health. I told him today I have been in the system twenty-one years and in those twenty-one years. I have only ever received three hours' help because my ten hours got cancelled. I think that's not fair. He explained that the job of a psychiatrist is only the biology of sickness, that's why it's just medication.

He also said that they cannot move on to a proper care plan until the person is stable. He read about my last visit with him last summer when I was elated then. I didn't go into psychosis because I have a good friendship network and my uncle Matthew told me to go to the doctor, your medication might not be right. I promised my uncle, I went straight away. My medication was changed, I have been able to cope till today really.

I told the psychiatrist I wish someone had told me all that twenty-one years ago. He explained it really well, so basically if you are not stable the care plan is not put in place because you are up and down, I told him I want to get to a place where I live in the middle. Is that possible.

Janet, first we have to get you stable. You're not having visits every six months anymore. We are going to keep a better look at you. We have to know how often you are elated, is it four times a year. More like four times since December.

He changed my medication back today to the tablets I was put on in Germany, I am so happy. Because I know they are better for me. And I told him why.

It's the old saying **"The truth will set you free"** I was so fearful of going into hospital I managed the situation for myself. This care plan has never been mentioned to me before. He said when you are stable, they will be putting in a care plan for me. I have been kept in the dark and it's all happening now. This book and a care plan to take me to the next part of my journey.

I take back some of the things I have said, let's just see who gets there first to the finish line, me or the system the race is on. I really wonder what my thoughts would have been for all these years if I had known about what I heard today.

It really makes me wonder. How stable do they want a person to be, I am thirty-four years in the same job, I have never missed paying any of my bills. If they never talk to you, what true picture are they getting, they only ever interviewed me when I was in psychosis. It's all very strange to me.

Why has this elation affected me this way?

I ended up jumping the gun, the thoughts in my head were ten years from now. I was thinking how big this book could become, thinking and seeing the way into the future. My little book would be printed, it would be in every English-speaking country, my thinking had even gone to a little flat in Germany.

My thinking had jumped ten years into the future and when you mix that type of thinking with no medication you become unglued. From true reality, my little book was no more than 43 pages on a computer, it hadn't even left my house yet. So, my thinking was irrational.

I was annoyed that the normal ways of dealing with elation did not work this time, I have decided that the next time this happens to me. I will be the person that tells me to go to the doctor. I am fed up with this elation affecting my job. At the same time, I am so happy that they always act fast and suggest for me to go see my doctor.

So, what did I learn from this experience, I was always an excitable person, as far back as I can remember? I was the child you couldn't tell that Christmas was coming because I would ask my ma how many more days and I would ask every day. It would kill me to wait. And when I was having fun with my cousins, I would go to bed still laughing and I would get everyone in trouble because I wouldn't settle.

In order to understand the person today we have to look back at the child you were yesterday, it shows you a good mirror image. I was an excitable child the elation happened for a reason this time.

I am standing in my way again with elation, I'm not allowing myself to come down. I have to put this into practice. Learn how to calm down. Stop holding on, allow the flow of the situation to come and go, there will be more funny moments this is not the only one, so, I need to let all things pass. I'm obviously handling it the wrong way.

Yes, I am excited to be writing all this down, the system has let me down, but I found my way through it all. I have to stay real in all situations. I need to learn to joke, tell a funny story and then calm down when the funny story is finished. I've been holding on to elated feelings. I've been holding on to a racing mind not letting myself sleep.

This is all the ego mind; it's been working overtime on me. This last year has been very hard on me, when I got rid of depression the energy kept me awake at night. It's like I was jumping from normal to high, normal to high. The ego mind was having a great time.

I'd get myself ready for bed even have a shower, go to bed. Say to myself it's time to sleep and an hour and a half would pass by, and I'd still be awake. My mind just wouldn't stop. So, I'd take the alarm clock downstairs with the duvet and pillow from the box room, I'd turn on the Television, I'd be asleep in two minutes.

This is the only thing that worked. I sleep in my bed most nights but with the help of sleeping tablets. I take my tablets and sleeping tablets at eight O'clock and at eleven I'm in bed. This is working, and I hope to do it without sleeping tablets in the future.

Both sides of Bipolar are profoundly serious, so serious that I needed to put what I learnt down on paper, I really do hope that you get something out of my journey, and I wish you all the best. On your journey of discovering your true path.

Nothing in my life needed to change, I needed to stop getting in my way and allow the true person in me to shine. And just start getting on with life.

Forgiveness and understanding.

I have come to a point now that whatever happened in the past stays in the past. Today is a new day and it needs to be given the respect it deserves. Every day the sun rises to greet us and bring us into a new day. When you have come to the point where you are able to give that respect to your days and enjoy them for what they are, that is where you are meant to be.

Do you have children, were no matter what went on the day before, no matter what they cried about, is all forgotten, and they smile as you wake them up in the morning. Well, when you learn how to drop the past, even getting out of bed becomes a joy, and you start to enjoy the new possibilities of the day to come.

Start your day the right way, did you have your Weetabix today, me I like to have a yogurt, and I love to have a coffee and a smoke and hop in my car and go to work. Not knowing what nice things could happen at work today.

I know this all seems very simple, but as you sit in the driving seat you control how you are, and you can put your best foot forward. You can smile and you can talk to people, and you never know what funny things could happen, so you enjoy your day.

Just meeting someone nice is the bonus, there are nice people everywhere.

Last Sunday I went to see my nieces new house, because it's a new set of houses and they don't have all their tenants yet. There is a man there to open the gates. He was friendly and he came quick to let me in. After I visited her lovely new house, I needed to get out of the gate again. He quickly came and we passed the time of day, then to say goodbye to him I cracked a joke, "I have to just call you Paddy" so he smiled and told me his name is Dave. Nice one, now if I go up to Leanne, I can say Hello Dave.

I have always loved to know people's names and people always like to tell me their names. Well, I only do this to people who work in shops that serve me. I do it all the time. I get smiles and even waves. I always leave room for a nice interaction. I love it.

Did I meet my need today, breakfast yes, dinner yes, tea yes, tablets yes?

I am a crazy lady, but in a nice way, during my depression I was not like this because I had lost my mojo, that was then this is now.

Forgiveness and understanding kind of come together, I am so happy today because I was able to bring forgiveness and understanding into my life. They are very important, they helped me to also forgive myself and bring understanding of all the situations I had experienced.

Yes, there are people that pushed and pushed to get their way. The things they done I could write another book, but it would only be my opinions, a one-sided opinion is not a clear story to tell, I needed all those stories or dramas in my life. They molded and shaped me to be who I am today.

I would not be who I am today without conflict. Conflict cracked me up and I kept opening the door to it, now I'm not saying to close your door to your family. Their ways helped me to change.

Me and my mother have been at logger heads for years. She is a very passionate women, she is very strong; she has the temperament of a passionate Italian women. She should have gone into acting. Instead, she does all her acting when she's with me.

It got to the point where today on the phone when she wouldn't allow me to finish my sentence, she's shouting at me, "your wrong", I'm shouting back at her "you're not letting me finish."

It's really funny, If I ring her tomorrow, it will be the same again, I've never told her this, but she might have a touch of confrontational disorder, we have some kids in our school there asked to do something, they refuse. Teachers sometimes have to shout at a child so that they do as they are told. I'm not saying my mother has confrontational disorder but it's funny that I'm always wrong, she gets so passionate, and she is the only one that is right. The shouting that has to go along with the conversation is funny.

I have pulled away from my mother all my life, I even wondered when I was a child, did I love my granny more. I felt understood by my Granny.

Love has expectations and every person has their own ideas on what love is, I continued wanting more from my ma, but her job was finished we are all adults. I needed to drop the expectations I had for my mother and just give space. She may be my mother, she is an individual, I need to show her the respect she deserves.

A funny thing happened a few days ago, I had had a screaming match with my mother, me being me I let her know this is what always happens. I say something, you tell me I'm wrong and we shout and scream at each other, it happens all the time. Two days later I called my mother, she was ready for me. You see she has known me since I was a baby, she has always known what buttons to press. She started talking about the covid 19.

I went up on my high horse, and I was shouting, and my mother sat there with an amused look on her face. She very coolly said to me, "Janet why are you shouting at me. It's so funny, she got me back for the telephone talk. She showed me it is not always her that there are two of us in it.

My mother was always prickly with me. I had a very simple idea about life. I was always trying to figure out life. My mother often got annoyed with my opinions. Even though she would be shouting at me, she would be showing me a different stance on life.

We didn't have a father rearing us, so my mother had to do everything for us. We had no washing machine then. My mother spent her Saturday mornings bent over the bath hand washing all our clothes and all the sheets from the beds, every floor was washed, everything was cleaned and polished. Saturday's, we got our pocket money and Sandra, Thomas and I would go visit our Granny Dunne. We'd leave our mother doing everything. We did help a little as we got older but only a little like clean our bedroom.

The first few years there was no money given to women that were in my mother's position. After two years it came, by then my mother was already working. Before my mother got the job the St Vincent de Paul, would give my Ma five pounds, my Granny Dunne would give my Ma two pounds, and my Granny Kelly would give my Ma one pound. That was all my mother had and the rent for our flat was two pounds. The rest of the money would need to be stretched.

My Granny Dunne was very clever, she said you come down to me every Saturday and I will have a big pot of stew on. And that will be one less dinner. She said go to your Ma on Sundays and that will be another dinner you don't have to cook or pay for, then you only have to have five dinners for you and the kids. And my Ma did what Granny Dunne said.

We loved Granny Dunne's stew the best, she had candy sauce and barley, and a big plate of bread and butter in the middle of the table. We loved dipping the buttered bread into the soup, we even made stew sandwiches. You always left the dinner table feeling full.

When Thomas started school, the St Vincent de Paul got my Ma into the local factory "Sambrafife", It was a great factory. They paid equal pay to men and women. My mother worked part time in the beginning. After a while my Ma went full time. She said at the time. We might not have a dad, but she might as well work full time because in this job she was able to bring in the money the same as a man.

We had two minders, and they minded us for two years. But after they had both left Ballymun because they got houses somewhere else. Then we looked after ourselves with all my mother's rules. Don't let anyone in the flat. Play with your friends till I come home, stay with the group, don't wander off and don't speak to strangers. Go to Mrs. O'Brien if you have any problems.

My Mother was twenty-five when her marriage broke down, family where always around or you visited your Granny's. My mother did her best, she was always late for everything, my mother would look like a film star. We were late for my Holy Communion, but my Ma looked great.

My Ma took us to Benidorm when I was eight. We were late for the plain and we had to run through the Airport, My Ma insisted at the duty free that she was entitled to buy something, the man said it was too late your plain is leaving. She insisted and she bought two packets of sweets. The plane waited and we were the last to board running across the airfield to catch our flight, as soon as we got on the plain, they closed the door. Safety belts on and the plane took off. My ma is funny, she had that argument, she got two packets of sweets.

My ma bought a motorbike so that she could be on time for work. She was always late, she would have to take a short cut through two fields and jump over a farmer's gate, one day she fell down on her Coxs, and her back was killing her, so she became the coolest mammy in Sillogue. Every evening at 5:30 she would come down Sillogue Road on her bike with a bag of messages. Sometimes the bag would burst, and the messages would be everywhere. We would always run to meet her with our friends. She would put one of us on the back of the bike and we'd drive around the back of our flat. My mother took the bike up to the second floor and parked it, in the end of our hall. (she put her bike in the lift).

We had the best mammy in the world, and she worked very hard. She never knew what she was coming home to and she would scream every day, when she'd walk into the kitchen. What the hell were they trying to cook.

The kitchen would be a mess, she'd have to clean it start dinner and wash up after dinner. Every day she would by a packet of biscuits, custard creams, orange creams or strawberry creams, this is how many were in the packet, Sandra would get three biscuits, Thomas would get three, I'd get three and my ma would get two. And that's exactly how many were in the packet. After dinner we'd have a cup of tea and our biscuits. It's a nice memory.

My ma did that because my ma had three little monster eaters, if she left anything in the press that could be eaten. We would eat it all when she wasn't looking and when she'd go to the press the packet might be there, but it would be empty. You'd hear her scream. So, she'd had to make new plans all the time. Ma always loved something sweet after dinner so that's why she would buy one packet of biscuits every day.

On Saturday morning you had to get to the supermarket early because they were only open a half day. So off we'd go, all four of us. With Thomas's baby pram to carry the messages in. My mother would do a big shop, for Saturday and Sunday. After shopping we would all be allowed to pick whatever ice pop we fancied, I loved Brunch and Golly bars. I was so busy eating my ice pop and loving it because it was great to be able to pick the one you wanted. I'd be Enjoying eating it, the whole world slipped away, even bringing the messages home slipped away, while I'd be enjoying that ice-cream.

My Ma had a lot to do on a Saturday and we were sent to my Granny's for the day. We played out in our Granny's. We'd stay there till the evening, then we'd be told we needed to go home.

Granny and Granda would give us some money, we didn't care Sandra would be given a little more because she was the eldest, Thomas and I would get the same. That didn't bother Thomas and me, money to buy sweets that's all that counted, we would stop at the first shop and spend it.

They loved us so much and they never forgot about us, they had lost their son Thomas, my father. And all they had from him was us, three little monsters. In our Granny Dunne's house, we could just be ourselves, run in, run out, the newspapers would be on the floor on a Saturday to keep the new clean floor clean for Sunday, My Granny had no time to sit and talk to you, she was always doing.

Saturday was a real working day for any women that worked, and my Granny worked in Gillesby's. She made lunches for the workers in the factory, and every day she'd have to clean the floor, the whole canteen floor. They all called her "Ma Dunne" because when the kitchen was closed, they'd try to come back to get more food or a tea or a coffee and she'd scream at them not to walk on the wet floor. It needed to look clean so it would be nice for the next day, Ma Dunne. She was a real mother. My Granny worked there till she retired, and she always said, if your Dad ever needed to contact me, he knows where I work. But he never did contact. He was missing.

He was her first child, he had shown his gifts as a child, His Granny and Aunt had sent him to learn the piano. He was so good that the piano teacher got him into the children's orchestra. He did many amazingly good things when he was a child that surprised my Granny when he was with my Ma, he did a lot of bad things.

My Granny and the other women that lived on her street all pulled together and they made life sweet for everyone. The women pooled together, they rented a twin tub and for 6 days it was passed around the houses. Every woman would have a day when they could do their washing. The machine was rented from a company, when the machine would break, the repair man would have to come and fix it. So, it was a perfect situation, it was running night and day. Only rented by one woman for all the women to use and the company knew nothing about the story of that machine and all that it did. They always had to fix it because it was rented.

Another great story, one of the days of the week the local Nun's ran a soup Kitchen and you could get a pot of stew for your family, for a very small price. My Granny would get her biggest pot for cooking a ham at Christmas. She'd send Tony and Maria her two young kids to the nuns with the money. And the nuns would have to give them a big portion because the pot was so big. My granny and the neighbor next door would share it and feed their families.

One day a few neighbors ran into my Granny, Thomas was on the back of a bike, with the boy that was, a bit touched. They were all afraid for Thomas. My Granny agreed with the women, she called for Thomas to come in and get off that bike. When my Granny had words with my dad, he was only little at the time. He said to my Granny. "He's entitled to have friends too." Out of the mouth of babes comes the truth. My Granny never stopped him again.

My Granny washed the bodies of anyone that died, and she'd be called for, this is something she never talked about, I just heard about it.

One day in my Granny's she had made a wedding cake, a three-tier wedding cake. It was on the table in the kitchen. She was putting all the fancy designs on it. I can still see it today in my mind's eye, truly amazing. Pure perfection not a mistake. She had great hands, she knitted in the evenings when she eventually sat down, she would be on her feet all day long. She never sat on a couch; she sat on a kitchen chair beside the fire.

Another thing about my Granny, she was an amazing cook, anything she made was so tasty. We made my ma make stew just like our Granny Dunne, we made our Ma buy candy sauce, we loved that on top of the stew. My Granny made a fry on a Saturday evening, most times we'd be going home at that time. All my uncles would all be tucking in, a big plate of buttered bread in the middle of the table. All you could see was one hand after another reaching in and grabbing a piece of bread. My Granny had four hungry boys to feed at that stage.

My Granda Dunne was a quiet man, he loved watching sport on television. He wasn't a chatterbox like me. He was a peaceful quiet man, he also made things. All the woodwork in my Granny's were made by my Grandad, he made pelmets for over the curtains. He made kitchen presses for my Granny, He built an extension at the back of the house, He always done the garden, he liked to go on Saturday evening for a pint and meet his friends. On Sunday evenings my Granny and Granda would go to the pub together, they were a united couple, and they loved each other. You never seen affection and we never got any hugs or kisses, but they truly loved us all. They are fondly missed by all of us.

I could keep telling you stories this is my last, my father was in the Orchestra, he would come home with different instruments and because he could read music, he'd be up in his bedroom mastering new instruments and my Granny would have to listen till he'd get it perfected.

Anyway, he invited a blind man from the orchestra to tea one Sunday. My Granny was a real worrier, "he won't be able to find the house, go meet him at the bus stop". My Dad said "No, he'll find the house". My Granny lined her children up, "Don't you dare say anything about the man been blind, don't you dare ask nosey questions". The man found the house no problem, and everyone sat around the table, the room was silent, the man had a funny watch, the front of it opened and every child was just looking how he felt the watch hands and he could see what time it was. They watched him as he moved his plate around. There was not one sound. Then the quietest man in Ireland spoke, my Granda said to the blind man, "isn't television a wonderful invention". My Granny laughed about that story till the day she died. She never told my Granda what not to say.

My Granny and Granda Kelly were different, their home was different, their ways were different. I have more memories from this side of the family, playing with my cousins, having fun, feeling safe.

There were more photographs from this side of the family, more childhood memories, family grooming, so to speak, how a person should act, how you should never pick your nose. It was a little house in the middle of Ballyfermot, and I loved going there my Granny Kelly would be so kind to children. I have great memories.

They placed a lot of their teachings on always going to mass, never give up on your faith. Well, a child that's looking for her way in the world, would be listening all the time. I know I was known as a little chatterbox, but I was intelligent, and I was listening too.

In the Kelly household I got a lot of my foundations, I told you my mother was always a bit prickly with me, well my Granny Kelly was not. She was abundantly kind to children. She understood the hearts and minds of children. She'd tell me little stories to help me understand.

I wasn't good at school, nobody tried to teach me, My Granny taught me all the other little things that helped you to get by in life. I baked with my Granny out in the back garden in the sunshine, I polished her lovely furniture with her. I'd go round to the shops with her list and the lady would write it in a copy book and my Granda would pay the bill another time.

We were always great eaters; my granny would always cook food that children loved to eat. Like sausages potatoes and peas, we would play with our dinner, make pictures with the food on our plates, my granny would allow us, but she would say to us, if you eat up all your dinner you can have jelly and ice-cream. We would eat up our dinner at that stage the food would be cold, we would lick the plate clean like a dog and we would get our jelly and ice-cream.

Everyone worried about my Granny because she had a bad heart. She lost her mother when she was ten years old to TB, and her little sister also died of TB. My Granny had a kind of sadness about her childhood. She died aged 69 in 1979.

My Granda Kelly was a lovely quiet man. He had a strong faith for God, he was bent over in his later years and he never complained about any pain he might have been in. He smoked a pipe and set beside the fire all day.

When we would come for a visit, he'd always ask Sandra and me to show him our Irish dancing, and we would do it for him, the funny thing was we only ever done the reel. He would give us his tobacco box; we'd put muck in it, and we'd play beds outside. He loved children, on Sunday's the ice-cream man would come and he'd get us all an ice-cream cone.

Because my ma worked so hard as we got bigger, we would get the two busses over to Ballyfermot and my mother would have the day to herself. My Granda would bring us into town and put us on the 36 bus. He loved going to the slot machines on the way, before he'd play, he'd buy us all a packet of Toffo. Some evenings my Granda would go to bingo, we thought this was funny because, we thought only women went to bingo. He lived to his 96th birthday. I don't remember the year that was.

This family had standards, standards my mother could not live up to, we were told. You're going over to Ballyfermot, don't be saying anything over there. They lived a high drama life and when they would hear the things, Sandra, Thomas and I had done on my Ma. They'd be compelled to help my ma.

That was the only reason why they told us how to be, they always told us to be good for our mother. That she worked really hard to keep us. I'd have to keep my mouth shut or I'd be in trouble with my mother.

Sandra, Thomas and I were really a handful for my ma, Thomas was the best brother a sister could want. We were only allowed two wish presents in a year, your Birthday and Christmas. Thomas was the baby and he'd cry if he couldn't have what the other boys had to play with because he wanted to play too. Pocket money wasn't enough money for the new skateboards all the way from America (made in Japan). I always remember walking out of the house laughing, I was going out to play with my friends and Thomas was crying for a skateboard.

We were playing downstairs and all of a sudden, here comes Thomas running with an aluminous bright green skateboard under his arm. he headed straight for the Hill he jumped on the skateboard and down he went, he had No Fear, he was able to go on a skateboard his first try. That's why he is so great to me. I went up to my Ma and asked could I have one too, she said a blunt No. you can share with Thomas, so to my memory we only ever had one skateboard in our house.

Thomas got other things other times when we didn't, it was always to play with. Thomas always had great ideas. It's his story not really mine to tell. He became a father years later and his children have had everything. He has really been a great father to have.

My Granny and Grandad tried to help my mother one time, Thomas was always attracted to where the fun was for a little boy, they taught. If they sent Thomas to school in Ballyfermot he'd do better, and he could come home every weekend.

Well, he turned into a little fat boy eating ice cream and jelly every day. He went to school and my Granny would have dinner ready for him, there is a school photo of Thomas, he had a big round face, he didn't look happy. He made friends on the road to play with and they turned out to be the same type of adventurous child that he was, he got too much for my Granny and Granda and he came home.

I really missed Thomas, our family felt strange without him at home, Sandra and I were jealous of the ice cream and Jelly every day, because we knew he'd get spoiled over there.

When Thomas came back to the block everyone was happy, all his friends missed him too. My mother put him in a new school and that suited him better.

My sister Sandra is the nicest person that I know, she's far from perfect. But if you could never laugh. She would help you to learn to laugh again.

She could get A's and Bs in school, and they put her in the best class in the school doing honor subjects and she left, she had to be dragged back to school to do her inter. Things were bad in our house at the time.

My sister was such a quiet child, she just plodded along, until a huge competitive streak came out in her, I think, if you could do that, she had to be able to do it too. She could climb trees, jump walls, skateboard, slide on the ice and she was good looking. She didn't know this till boys got interested in her in her teens.

She fell hopelessly in love in her teenage years. I didn't understand this, I didn't understand. I knew she loved hard. She is very funny really and crazy at the same time.

There was always a bit of competition between Sandra and me. We are not always on the same page but when we are in our giddies, we are really very funny together. It doesn't happen all the time but there's always the next time.

Sandra understands me more then I understand her. She has said the odd remark to me, and she was always right on the money.

Growing up in Ballymun was great, our school was just across the road from our flat. We had a phone box in front of our flat, we had green space and an under tunnel with hills that when the snow would come, we'd all be sliding down those hills having great fun. At the back of our flat we had an all-weather pitch with two tennis courts. When I was eight years old, they built a swimming pool right next to the shopping center.

The 36 was our bus, the bus stop was right beside our block, you only had to cross the road to catch the bus into town.

I loved the families that lived on our block, there were big families and small families, but they all had something we loved, their Kids.

Hello Mrs. Malone, hello Mr. O'Brien, hello Mrs. Brant, Hello Mr. O'Connor.

When me and my friend Paula would be in the lift, we'd say hello to the Adult that was in the lift, but then you'd say nothing, and they would say nothing and up you'd go with the adult to their floor. Complete silence would always make two little chatterboxes burst out laughing, we wouldn't even make it to the second floor without laughing, it was a little game we'd play.

"What floor do you want" we'd know the floor, but we always had to ask, just in case they wanted a different floor. It would go like this, "Hello Mr. O'Connor, what floor would you like" and we'd press the button for him. We had to stop playing that game because we couldn't stop laughing. We were two little titters together.

That was Paula, the funniest friend I ever had, she was also the most inventive friend I ever had, in my house there wasn't too much laughing, in Paula's they were always laughing and getting up to something new. Paula and I would double dare each other. She was a great friend; I have always missed our friendship. We were both in two different year groups and we had a different group of friends, but we had great times and memories of the Blind disco, cycling, always going on adventures.

There are so many, many stories and funny things I be here forever. I hope you have the picture. Things weren't bad, I was having a nice life in Ballymun.

I don't want to talk about Tommy too much, he was violent with my mother, and she didn't deserve that, she had been a good mother. What we got introduced to, really affected us to the point where, he died, and Sandra and I never went to the funeral. I do forgive Tommy after all I did go to him for advice, He was an intelligent man. I copied him and I delt with problems the way he would. I didn't find my own way.

He was a good man really, but he had a violent streak. We were all greatly affected by my Ma's and Tommy's relationship.

Bobby and Oonagh are his children from his marriage, they are lovely. Bobby lived with us, and Oonagh came for long holidays from school because her mother worked. Oonagh was only six years old when she came and I was about fourteen, I got to know her, she was a real Daddy's girl, she was a very playful child, she came everywhere with me when I was around.

Bobby was the same age as Sandra, and Sandra didn't like that, they were in the same year in school. This was very uncomfortable for Sandra. Nobody had ever asked Bobby how he felt.

I really liked Bobby, he had great friends, he loved his music, he caught me dancing in the sitting room thinking I was some sort of film star. We both had respect. Bobby did well for himself in life, I think he has traveled around the world at this stage and like me for some strange reason he never had kids.

Philip was the best little baby, I played with him a lot and I took his places. We watched Bosco together every day. I would get him all excited. He was a funny baby. Philip was watching a wildlife program and he seen gorillas for the first time, and he burst out laughing, as they picked flees off each other and rolled on the ground. Philip laughed his head off. He was about two years old.

Philip was a very good child. When he went to school my mother decided to send him to the best school. The Irish school on the Ballymun road. Learning didn't come easy to Philip. He loved his classmates, I think because he had no little brother or sister to play with, he became the class clown, and he was learning very little. He made his Holy Communion in the Irish school, but after he had to go to an English-speaking school. He went to the Virgin Mary School in Shangan, my Ma lived in the flats. When He made his confirmation, his mother and Father had truly split up.

I was living in Germany at that time, when I came home there was a whole new Philip, he was bold, cheeky, greedy and he just wasn't the same little boy. He was making his mother and father jump through hoops. He was angry and demanding for all his wants. He had stopped being the good little boy he once was.

I loved Philip so much this was hard, my mother gave him everything, not buying food to get him the runners he wanted. She had a hard time with him. At fourteen he stopped going to school he would go but he would run out and throw a chair.

He was in the Comprehensive school at the time, my mother was there too, because she went back to do her Leaving Cert. My ma made a mistake in my opinion.

The school wanted him back, they knew he needed help, and they were willing to work with him. They always have a child that after a marriage breakdown hits out at everyone.

Philip had lots of friends, and they all were drinking and smoking hash. When they had the money. This became his life. As far as I know all his friends came good, but Philip didn't, and many years later he was smoking heroin. He loved me and I loved him, but I never accepted the path he was on. He felt very judged by me. Janet lived to standards.

I could not accept the situation he was in. I did help him; When he would take the time to come over to me for money, he was always lucky. My purse would always have what he needed he only came a few times. I bought him three coats in his life, I would bring him over some messages, and I cut his hair.

This was not the life I wanted for him, with the drugs he lived a lot with voices in his head and in the end, he had to come home to my Ma's, he spent the last two years of his life in comfort, he was on medication for schizophrenia, these did help him but the voices where still there, he overdosed, he is one year dead at 38 years of age.

Such a sad existence, he had so many struggles with himself, he lived in his head all the time and the voices would start nice, he had two voices in his head a woman and a man and they would tell him he was stupid, they would tell him how bad he was, they would torment him really.

I did go to Father Peter McVerry for help for Philip, we had a nice talk, he gave me a number Philip would have to ring, he will have to make this phone call himself, you can't do this for him.

Another place I contacted was a place in the Wicklow mountains. They gave me a number too, but Philip needed to want to help himself. He explained about addiction that as soon as Philip would ring, they would get him started and help him. That he has to come to that point himself.

He also said the addiction was so hard because when you wake, you want to give up drugs, you need help fast that later the addiction is so strong that you have to take more, you hate that you actually have to take more.

We had many family crises after my ma met Tommy.

The chain of events, the circumstances that followed and the length of years. My mother was fourteen years in and out of that relationship. Philip was twelve at that stage, I had gone through a marriage breakdown. Jumping the years to Twenty-seven. I took a career break, and I followed Thomas to Germany.

I spent two golden years in Germany, I was away from all family stresses. I had the time of my life, I learnt to speak German. I loved the place I lived in and so did Thomas, he was having a ball too.

I came back home; Thomas went on to live in Australia and rear a beautiful family.

Sandra and I seemed to jump into relationships and get burnt, I'd help Sandra but there was always another problem. Because I didn't mind my own business. Something else would always seem to happen.

I'm getting a bit sick telling you the story, long story short, I ended up in St Brendan's a mental institution. I'm calling it an institution because some people I met there have been there since they were teenagers.

I'm only going to talk about my first visit. This for me is a very dark story and I don't really know how to start.

Please remember all the good things I have talked about. I told you already that I was a bag of stress running from pillar to post. I was only good at cleaning and saving money to get the things I wanted, I told you I had so much to learn, that I really knew nothing much about true love and self-love. Because I didn't understand the basic things in life, I could be sucked into any Drama. I thank my mother for the beautiful childhood I remember and my Granny's too. Being an adult, I found it hard.

I ended up in St Brendan's, (grange Gorman) a child in our family was very sick indeed, she could have died. Thank God today she lives in Australia she has three Kids; she is married, she has put down roots there.

The way my family was handling the situation and how overwhelming it was, I went into grief. A little too much that I lost my reason. I have always loved Children and when someone hurts a child it affects me greatly, even to this day.

Anyway, I couldn't handle the realities, and I jumped into a psychosis, for the first time. I was so upset. I wasn't right in the head as they say. I walked from Crumlin, my auntie's house to where my grandfather was in hospital. Cherry Orchard. I was in psychosis, I walked the canal the early hours of the morning, I made my way up to see my grandfather, I was on my way to Italy to my cousin Dawn, My Dawning of the day. That was how my head was working. I got to the Hospital, I had no idea of time, I had started walking in the dark and after some time it was bright, the traffic was getting heavy. I was going to walk to Italy.

I got to the hospital, and I got the numbers mixed up and I went to the wrong house, the hospital has four or five little bungalows or houses. I went to the wrong door, and I asked to see Jim Kelly.

They said he was not there. How dare they keep me from seeing the head of my family. I thought they were lying so I burst right through them. I started running into all the rooms looking for my grandfather. He wasn't in them.

Where were they hiding him? What have they done to him? I was in a complete panic. I went into a darkened room, there was a disabled man in a wheelchair his head was so big, I looked in shock at him then I kissed him and came out by then the police where there.

I'm not telling anymore, it's enough; the rest of the story would only turn it into a comedy. And it was no comedy. It's really only for my friends that are able to laugh because I have done many things through the years.

Police station, police cell, doctor called and taken to St Brendan's, do you like the way I shortened that. Well sometimes it's important to keep something to yourself.

Dignity, how it gets taken away.

In St Brendan's, I had to wait to see the psychiatrist. When I got brought into his office, he interviewed me, what was said. I really don't remember being psychotic at the time everything was surreal.

After the interview I was asked to follow a male nurse nicely, I was brought to a ward, brought into another office and interviewed again.

I was asked to follow a nurse, a lady, I did, all of a sudden, I was in a padded cell I was pushed to the ground on a mattress that was on the ground, I was manhandled by what seemed six nurses.

My clothes were dragged off me, my underwear too. I was screaming. Some were on top of me holding me down. My psychosis made me imagine a gas mask and I could even smell the gas, I heard me scream, the most horrific cry I had ever heard in my life come out of me, it sounded like an animal from the deepest forest deep down in my soul, and I screamed these words to the bitches.

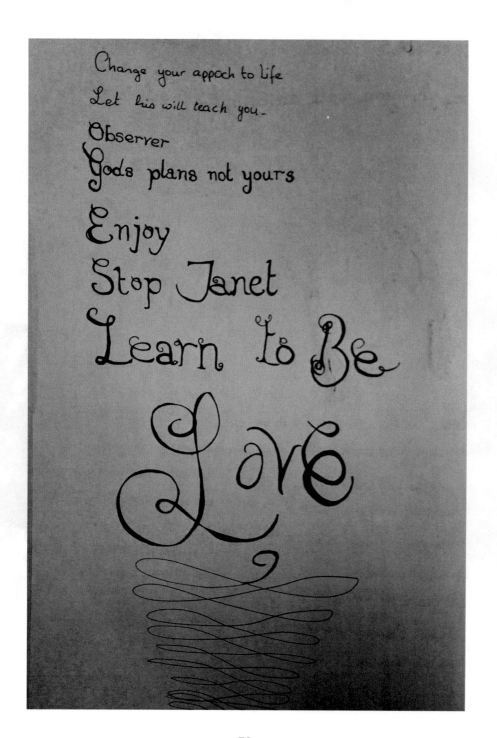

Change your appoch to life

Let his will teach you.

Observer

Gods plans not yours

Enjoy

Stop Janet

Learn to Be

Love

♥ Always Be Willing to Change ♥

♥

You may be Sad

And need to cry

Tear's you cannot hold.

Let them go, relece them!

You do not always need to be brave!

Tear's wash the overload of your heart

You will be happy another Day ♥

Remember Always

Sadness passes

Tommorow could be your

Greatest Day ♥

NOW I KNOW WHAT YOU DID TO THE JEWS.

I was knocked out till the next day, who knows was it the next day. I woke up naked lying on the mattress. The mattress had no sheets on it, there was this huge, big dress, as thick as a coat you would wear in a Blizzard, it was like something from an orphanage.

The room was locked, you had no facility to go to the bathroom, there was a cardboard toilet in the corner. There were three cameras looking straight down on you naked. They didn't let you out till you used that paper toilet. After I used the paper toilet a key turned in the door, the door was open slightly. Nobody was there. I made my way up the corridor to a room at the end, it was the common room where all the patients were. The dress was like a cotton sack. Thank God it wasn't horse's hair. I was in shock, and I could remember everything, just not the words in the interview.

Now I'm out, they have done their worst to me. I complied with everything, but they were not finished. Next came their medication.

I couldn't control the saliva in my mouth, I was dribbling. After a few days I couldn't talk my tongue would not move at all and I could hardly get the spit in my mouth to swallow. They had to take me off a tablet called Serinase.

The real toilets where full of shit, nobody cleaned them. I was so bored, I hate dirty toilets so, I cleaned them. Not even the cleaner that came every day cleaned them. It was a disgrace. Your days were so long there, you had nothing to do, and no nurses talked to you, they spent their time in the kitchen drinking tea and talking to each other.

I got to know the stories of a few girls one girl was in there since she was Seventeen. One lady would swallow spoons Knives and forks, when she would get sicker. She told me her story and when she done that she'd have to be sent to a real hospital, have an operation to get them out.

Well, one night she was not herself, a strange look came over her face, she wasn't talking to me or anyone else. I did ask her if she was ok, she just stared blankly a head. The Nurse's noticed nothing they were always in the kitchen. That lady had swallowed a spoon, a tablespoon not a teaspoon. She just sat there.

When it was time for medication the nurses all came out together, and they were giving us our tea. When the lady wouldn't take a sandwich, and she was just blankly staring. Then there was panic. Two of the nurses dragged her out of the room, I never seen her again.

I seen a few more things too, you are talking about people who have been hurt in life, so hurt that just been friendly and telling their story, could have been too much for them, we don't know what has made that person get a mental illness. That is why you have to be your best friend and do kind things one by one.

In the mornings I would always make my own bed. Funny enough, the nurses would come in and make the beds that were not made. But they left the toilets filthy. And the floors were cleaned every day, but the toilets?

That's enough about all that... I did get out, but it was a three month stay. It took me a year to recover. They were treating me for schizophrenia, they never told me. I was like a zombie. If my hand went up in the air to say something my friend would push it down, I'd be talking, and my hand would still be in the air. I couldn't hold conversations; my friends Alison and Josephine were great to come and visit me. Really there is so much credit needed to give to these two girls cause that's all they were then. Today they are hitting their forties, but then they were only twenty years old. They had to break away from me and my Bipolar the first ten years were spent up and down, I always tried my best.

When I was a little better, I thought maybe I should go to Mary Pender for some acupuncture. That same afternoon my speech came back, I was feeling normal, I rang my ma, I was so delighted and so able to speak.

The next time I had a visit with the psychiatrist, my Ma came with me, she ate them, for the medication they had me on. They decided it was Bipolar because I was able to get better, if they had kept me on the tablets for schizophrenia who knows where I'd be today.

Relax, no more bad stuff, it happened more times to me but that's enough about that. In the beginning I told you all the good stuff. That is what's real. It was the most horrible experience of my life. Especially the treatment in the padded cell by the Bitches. They took away my dignity. They knew no better. They took my Jewelry and never gave me back my sentimental stuff.

Please excuse my Language, Fuck it. It really happened and It really happened to me. I have a life to live, that story was twenty-one years ago this September -October. I will never look for those files, what they did was disgraceful. How they treated people they will be ashamed of all their lives. I'm not interested.

I only met a few nice nurses when I was there, that I would call nice people. The rest were social climbers only in it for the money, and the patients are taught nothing, nothing about mental health.

I actually don't know how to finish; I'm not cured yet. If I have my way I will be cured and by writing all this, you hopefully getting something out of it. There may be something in it for both of us. Shit happens, it's just shit. Flush the toilet. (They can clean their own toilets now).

You make sure to make one change in your life that you can. Be kind to yourself. As you get better, life will pick up. Nothing really worked for me till I stopped self-criticizing.

AS THEY SAY, TAKE A LEAF OUT OF MY BOOK, WIPE YOUR TEARS AWAY. I have no self-pity. I did, but now I don't.

All people have different experiences in life to teach them lessons, it doesn't matter what life throws at us, even if it pulls us down to the bottom of our existence. We are always meant to stand up and be counted with the rest of mankind.

Standing up again as quick as we can, it took 21 years for me and the solutions where all so easy in the end. It was a hard road one I will never truly forget. As my Granda Kelly would sometimes say, let bygones be bygones. The simple things in life are free, the simple kindness you do for yourself makes you strong again.

Put yourself first.

I told you I always missed my father. Well, when I was twenty-five, I had a dream, I wrote a poem to my father in the dream, to tell him how much I loved him. Unconditional love. This dream was a real gift from the dream world to me. I ran downstairs and I only had four lines left from that dream, the first four lines.

Thomas ....Da

You were my first love.
You were my first face.
Our love was never lost.
It was just a bit misplaced.

Screaming into the world I came
And you came running in
You looked to your surprise.
A newborn baby wide awake

You were my first love.
You were my first face.
Our love was never lost.
It was just a bit miss placed.

We love our parents unconditionally even if they are not around. Nothing and nobody are perfect. Nature is perfect, your true nature is perfect for you alone, if that's not good enough, there is something amiss, you are perfect just as you are.

I'm leaving you now, to do the work and find your own way.

- **Be kind and cheerful. Everyone has problems you can't see.**

This book has only one intention, to help someone in the same position as myself find ways to help themselves. Everything that I wrote about really worked for me. Bipolar started for me when I was thirty-four. So, I had lived a lot of life before I snapped.

I was in my job fourteen years; in those years I had got married and I had bought my own house. I had traveled to a few European countries, took a career break, lived in Germany. After my marriage broke down, I had lodgers living in my house to help me have some extra money, my wages were just not enough to pay my bills. After about seven years doing that there was a big pay rise and I didn't need lodgers anymore. Two of the lodgers Seve and Nuria still have contact with me today, and they come to visit, Seve comes to Ireland every year, he always helps in my house.

I have friends since I was a teenager the ladies that I babysat for, Anna and Teresa and their families and my family aunts and uncles. I have a friend in work Carmel, she is the same age as my mother, we have worked together for the last 38 years. I have a good friend in Germany that I have always kept the contact with Dani, she is great fun. I have a few cousins too that are my friends, really Dawn and Paula. They have always been there for me. I have always been there for all these friends and family too.

If I am out of sync, my friends and family will let me know.

I know what depression looks like and I will not accept it in my life. I also know when I'm in elation, and I act fast, if I can't control it, I will take myself to the **psychiatrist.**

It is all a big learning curve, one that we have to hold ourselves responsible for.

Sorry I taught I was finished

Loneliness

Lonely yes, I did feel lonely, when I was stuck, I was lonely, I had spent years holding on to one dream, this brang loneliness into my life. The dream to be happily married, this dream was in my head always. I rationalized the idea in my mind saying, well you have to get yourself better and maybe its better this way. Lying on the couch and not having energy and no real will to live. Maybe it's better this way.

But I still held on to the dream. I have been reading a lot of self-help books, watching a lot of people on the internet teach you about life. I don't remember where I got this, but they were right.

I lived a life as a single woman, my dream of the perfect life was with someone I could share my days and life with. My dream was unrealistic, to the circumstances that I found myself in. and this dream was making me feel very lonely indeed. I had to drop the dream and get realistic. My dream was not my life, my life was that of a single woman and I had to enjoy it for what it is.

Also, by having that as a dream, it was also helping me to forget what I do have, and it allowed me to live in my head. Living in your head dreaming, ok we do have dreams when we sleep, they are real dreams, I'm not talking about real random dreams, there great you never know what they are about. I'm kind of talking about a wish dream that you think of from time to time, a daydream that you conjure up. This robs us of accepting things as they are.

I am a single woman still, and I have only one plan for my future, and that is to stay well mentally, have a nice life, appreciate all that is around me, dreams do come true, but it would be very sad if I took my daydream any further. My life is so special to me now, I lost a lot of years. And my dreaming made me lonely.

It was not easy to lose that dream, but as I accepted things as the truly were and appreciated all that I had in my life, friends and family, I was really doing well.
Writing this book has truly helped me, it has reminded me of all the happy memories of my childhood. I know things were not perfect, but the memories are all so funny.
During the first lockdown I spent three months with my Ma, it was great to see how easy going that passionate woman really is. She was getting over a knee operation, so I did the shopping for us, we had great sunshine, and her little garden is a real sun trap. I loved going out in the mornings with my coffee.

The lockdown also gave me time for me. I didn't have to rush into a job and forget about yourself and it just slowed me down, I was running over to my house to do the garden, that grass just kept growing like it does every year. Staying in my Ma's was good. We had harmony and we got on really good.

The shouting started again, but it was a little funny. She never goes anywhere, she has her two clubs, they are cancelled because of the lock-down, she misses them. They are her only out in a week. She considers herself the head of the family and she expects us to call to see her. That's just the way she is.

She relaxes in her own space in her own company. There is a lesson in that as well.

True authentic personality

When we place a true value on our existence. When we realize we are important to ourselves, and we live the life we have in a true manner. We stop neglecting ourselves. We truly learn we are important, everyone around us is important too.

When we realize this, the new life begins, we smile and laugh because it was only our thinking that needed to change. Life becomes fun again.

Taking the mask off, it's really funny the masks I wore to live up to the standards of other people, what I thought the world wanted to see, I was wrong.

You may need to have a mask on in certain situations but only for a short time, being yourself is really grounding. It's really good to know who you really are. I was mad about cleaning to keep up to other people's standards. It is nice to have your home in order but when you relax you keep it tidy because you want it like that, and you clean it when you are in the right frame of mind.

Just being yourself is enough, holding on to the ideas of others stopped me from truly being myself, so that all had to go, who am I, I am an experience of life, I enjoy my days each one is special, you never know what the day will bring.

I listen to my body, if I get tired, I sleep, if I am hungry, I eat, isn't it funny that a life I had made so complicated, could be so simple now. The simplicity of life now makes it all the more interesting.

Plans are made to get broken did you ever hear that. All my plans got broken, it was for the better, now I am a woman sitting on the seat of her existence driving my life to who knows where, nobody knows the end of the story.

I wish the readers of this little book everything.

God Bless you
Janet.
Completed 15/09/2024

To the reader that doesn't understand Bipolar

Bipolar is a chemical imbalance, this is how it has been explained to me, the chemicals in your brain don't cap, so when you go high you can't stop going higher than the norm. When you are in a depression you go deeper than the norm.

I am a deep thinker and always have been,

Mental illness came into my life at the age of 34, it was always there but for many years my brain could handle itself. We had a family tragedy. I couldn't handle the situation or the grief I found myself in and I went into a psychosis. I lost touch with reality; in a matter of days, I was in a mental Hospital. I was utterly shocked when I woke up in that hospital. But my real journey started when I tried to resume my life.

While in hospital I met a lot of people that were very sick, so just to explain to you how and why it happened to me is my story. But the circumstances of others I cannot speak for. I met people that had been sexually abused in their childhood and when they reached their teens they were put into this mental hospital. I met people that self-harmed, they would seem ok but when their mood changed, they put their hand through a window. I helped a girl one day that was committing suicide by tying a band around her neck, I ran into her cell and held the band away from her throat. I shouted for the nurses, they all came running in and pushed me out of the way. I never seen that girl again. That happened when I was in the observation unit, I got moved to the normal hospital. Where I met more people, more stories. Not one story was the same, but we were all there for one reason to get well.

The real struggle starts when your back in your life, the medication took a very long time to get into my system. I walked around like I was a zombie, stiff and slow, I needed sunglasses because I found the sun too bright, it took me about 6 months before I felt normal. There are some family photos of me at that time and my eyes looked strange in all the photos. I have got on with my life as good as I could, worked and been with my family and friends, at the same time carried around a sunken feeling inside. I surfed on their stories while I hid my true feelings. Never open about my depression because if I had died, I would have been happy. My depression it is gone a long time now. Thanks to the people I reached out to for help. I still to this day can go into elation. I do my best to put rules there, so I can stay in control. It's not always that easy. But the things I taught myself really worked for me.

It has taken many years to come to this point in my life, I know that depression is a wish for death because we go into it too deeply, it's like you are in a black hole you can't find your way out. I lay on my couch a lot and did very little except watch TV. To live normal was a very big struggle. I had always been a person to enjoy my life but when I found myself in this situation I wasn't enjoying it.

I read a lot of books, and I listened to youtubers to help me. I went to church a lot; I joined a lot of clubs just to keep me from Lying on the couch. Nothing ended till I accepted the situation and started to become my one and only best friend.

As I learnt things that truly worked for me, I would share with my friends and family. Most times I shared; people were not interested because they wanted to sort their problems out for themselves.

The Night Paddy told me he was suicidal, I told him about Micheal Murphy and what he had told me to do for a dark spirit, it had worked for me. Paddy took that on board and a few weeks later he told me it really worked, and he was ok. So, I learnt you can only give help when the person comes to you with a problem, they want help with it, but when someone is just telling you how they are feeling, just listen. They need to figure it out for themselves if they want the situation to change.

I carried being Bipolar very hard, I had squeezed myself out of my existence so to speak. I knew how to look after everybody else, but I had to teach myself to look after myself. I still have areas in my life that could improve, like going for a walk. Getting out in the fresh air. That will all change in time, in my job I get enough exercise so I'm not worried.

This is a very tricky area and from my experience a very long road because you have to change, that change didn't come easy. There was no quick fix.

Printed in the United States
by Baker & Taylor Publisher Services